HIGH PEAKS
ENGINEERING

"Nothing is too small to know, and nothing is too big to attempt."

—WILLIAM CORNELIUS VAN HORNE

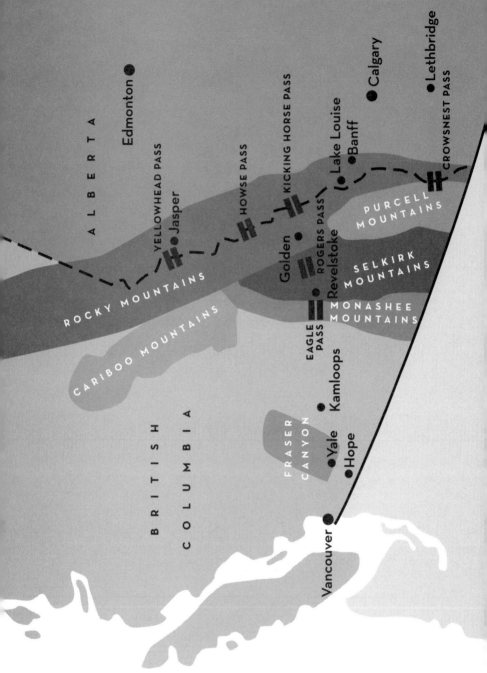

The major mountain ranges and mountain passes of southeastern British Columbia.

Contents

Prologue

YOU ARE AWAKENED IN THE early-morning darkness by a shrill blast from a locomotive whistle. You lurch out of your bedroll and stride to the cook tent with a throng of other men for a stomach-filling breakfast of greasy flapjacks, bacon, and a brown liquid masquerading as coffee. You join your assigned crew, check in with the paymaster, and pick up your tools to start another day of manual labour at the end of a track in the middle of nowhere. Each man has his assigned task. Using rudimentary hand tools—crowbars, axes, sledge-hammers, and hand drills—they move gravel, break up rocks, cut down trees, and level the rail bed. Teams of horses pull wagons loaded with wooden ties and massive nine-metre iron rails weighing in at 450 kilograms each. These are unloaded with caliper-type tongs at regular intervals along the rail bed. For each kilometre of track, 1,560 ties must be laid. Only the toughest men survive.

There are hundreds of men in every line crew, with each line divided into three sub-crews that progress sequentially toward the horizon. Work is organized down to the smallest detail under the eagle eye of a supervisor. Civil engineers have already laid out the transcontinental rail route, and the right-of-way has been marked by surveyors whose job is to "spy out the line," calculating placement, curves, and elevations. The grunt work of construction begins with clearing crews who are out front removing obstacles like trees, roots, and boulders. Trees are cut down and used to build trestles and the telegraph poles that parallel the rail line. If possible, boulders are rolled out of the way, but this can be dangerous. Once rolling, the boulders can drag men and mules down the slope and crush workers below. Huge stumps, hillsides, and rock faces are blasted apart using black powder in a process called "grubbing." Black powder, a variation of gunpowder composed of charcoal (carbon), saltpetre (potassium nitrate or sodium nitrate), and sulfur, is replaced over time by dynamite, which is three times more powerful, and finally by highly unstable liquid nitroglycerin. At a detonation, whether intentional or accidental, crews must take cover from airborne rocks and spears of flying wood. Some aren't fast enough and are injured. Wounds are bandaged and work continues. When a labourer is killed, he is buried nearby. Workers claim that for every kilometre of CPR track, a nameless immigrant lies buried along a riverbank or in the bush. Only a flimsy wooden cross or flag marks his final resting place. The foreman inspects the work in each section, then yells for the men to toss their tools into the wagons and move up to the next section to do it all over again.

Last but not least, the rail-setting crews bring up the rear. Ties of cedar, pine, and tamarack have been hewn from tree trunks flattened on the top and bottom to measure 2.5 metres long by 2.5 centimetres deep by 25.5 centimetres wide. In a precisely orchestrated drill, two men lift each tie into place on the rail bed, exactly 46 centimetres apart. They are followed by six men, three per side, who hoist 9-metre rails imported from the UK and Germany up out of wagons. The rails are lowered into place exactly 1.4 metres apart in compliance with standard rail gauge, the distance between the wheels of rolling stock. Men called "spikers" then pound 18-centimetre spikes into the ties to hold the rails in place. Three sledgehammer blows per spike gets the job done all the way up the line.

Nobody has it easy. Labourers travel light. Personal items are few—just the clothes on their backs and maybe a pocket knife, deck of cards, or harmonica. Nothing is safe from petty thieves, so they keep their pay in their pockets at all times— that is, the money remaining after recreational time spent around the campfire or kerosene lamp. Following a dinner of beef, beans, potatoes, bread, and coffee, the men gamble, sing, smoke, or drink, although alcohol is restricted because *of the fights it can cause. The men are from many European nations, and few can read or write. There are not many letters home. They are here because even though the work is brutal, you do get paid a reasonable wage for manual labour. But your salary of $20 to $26 a month is reduced for non-work days, which include Sundays and stoppages caused by inclement weather, delayed supplies, or being too sick to work. Medical care is rudimentary at best. Constructing the transcontinental rail line is not a job for the faint of heart.*

CHAPTER

1

From Colony to Confederation

THE COLONY OF BRITISH COLUMBIA is isolated. It is separated by mountain, prairie, and Precambrian Shield from the colony of the "United Canadas," formerly Canada East (now Quebec) and Canada West (now Ontario). But Sir James Douglas (a.k.a. "Black Douglas" because his mother was reportedly Creole), chief factor of the Hudson's Bay Company (HBC) and later governor of the Colony of Vancouver Island and the Crown Colony of British Columbia, has a dream: a continental land link between the two settlements. It would bind them together, and none too soon.

Thousands of American prospectors had arrived at the Fraser and Thompson Rivers in 1858, hoping to strike it rich in the Cariboo gold rush. Fearing US expansion north of the forty-ninth parallel, Douglas took action to assert British sovereignty. On August 2, legislation was passed by the British colonial office designating the HBC-administered territory as the new Colony of British Columbia. Its capital would be New Westminster, near the mouth of the Fraser River. Douglas then sought to populate the colony with settlers from the very country that had provided the rowdy problem miners.

He sent word south to California, where a number of free blacks and former slaves were looking for a place to settle. The group sent a delegation to Victoria to investigate, who returned with glowing reports about the attractiveness of the region. Soon after, four hundred black pioneers set sail from San Francisco on the ship *Commodore* for a new life where they would have the right to vote, sit on juries, and, after seven years, become British citizens. They quickly established themselves and formed a solid core of retail and farming businesses. Later on, several took an interest in discussions to negotiate the colony's entry into Confederation in 1871.

Douglas decided to promote colonial commerce by building a better supply road through the rugged canyon country of the Interior. It would run 644 kilometres, from Fort Yale through the Fraser Gorge, northward to Quesnel, and eastward to Williams Creek. Douglas was sympathetic to the harrowing tales of miners who risked their lives, not to mention their fortunes, crossing whirlpools, First Nations trails, narrow ledges, and steep precipices on foot.

He appointed his friend Alexander Anderson to supervise construction.

This Great North Road, also known as the Douglas Trail, Lillooet Trail, Harrison Trail, and Lakes Route, would be the primary route to the goldfields of the BC Interior. Initial surveys for the road in 1858 were conducted by the British Corp of Royal Engineers, also called "sappers," who completed the two most difficult stretches, from Yale to Boston Bar (ten kilometres) and on to Cook's Ferry along the Thompson River (fifteen kilometres). Much of the road-bed had to be blasted into existence from solid rock. The rest of the route would be completed between 1859 and 1861 by local construction crews. To help finance the trail, Douglas had five hundred men deposit $25 each, a substantial sum back then, to guarantee they would work to the end and not abandon the project when the going got rough. For his part, Douglas would provide pack mules, equipment, and food. When the job was done, the workers' deposits would be returned and their supplies delivered to the goldfields. Yes, the men got their money back, but the promised mules never arrived, and the men had to carry all the supplies and equipment themselves for the entire construction period.

But the colonists wanted a better route from Fort Yale to the goldfields at Barkerville. While the Douglas Trail was useful, it could not handle much freight. So, from 1862 to 1863, a new, improved Cariboo Wagon Road was built. Using picks, shovels, and black powder to break up rock, crews of

A wagon road in British Columbia's Fraser Canyon, *circa* 1860s.
GLENBOW ARCHIVES NA-674-58

labourers framed bridges and blasted out footings from the steep sides of the Fraser and Thompson Rivers. At 5.5 metres wide, the completed road to Barkerville would be wide enough for two double-hitched horse teams to pass. Some entrepreneurial contractors received cash subsidies from the colonial government to build the road and, when it was complete, were allowed to charge tolls for its use. But not all endeavours were so lucrative. When government payments were delayed, contractors had to put up their own money to finance construction, and many abandoned the hard work for the dream of instant riches in the goldfields. Others hoped to make their money in supply management. One group invested in twenty-three Bactrian (two-hump) camels, bought for $300 each from the US Camel Corps, for use as pack animals on road construction. Estimated profit: $60,000 a year. After all, they reasoned, camels can carry twice as much and go twice as far per day as mules. The camels travelled from Arizona, where they had been part of a desert survey mission, to San Francisco, where they set sail on the steamer *Hermann* to Victoria. An article in the May 29, 1862, edition of the *British Colonist* newspaper stated, "They are now acclimated and will eat anything from a pair of pants to a bar of soap." However, the cut-rock trails hurt their soft foot pads, and many camels went lame in spite of being outfitted with rawhide and canvas booties. Also, they bit, kicked, and were more ornery than the mules. In addition, their pungent odour alarmed the horses and mules, who often stampeded when they caught a whiff of their competition. The camels were eventually set free or sold at a loss to ranchers as exotic pets. The last known survivor, called The Lady, died around 1900 while living near Grand Prairie (now Westwold), BC. And so ended the great Canadian Bactrian boondoggle.

Mule trains, covered wagons, stagecoaches, and even oxen used the precarious passages to Barkerville. Inns and stables sprung up every fifteen to twenty kilometres along the two routes, providing food, lodging, and fresh horses.

In just one year, $6.5 million worth of gold travelled via the wagon roads from the Interior to the coast. By 1864, both interior routes were operational and advertising in local newspapers. An ad for the Great North Road/Douglas Trail started with "Hurrah for the Cariboo! Douglas and Lillooet route is by far the shortest for both animals and men." An ad for the Cariboo Wagon Road claimed, "Every person should know that the shortest, best, and cheapest route to the Cariboo Mines is via the Yale and Lytton Wagon Road." Eventually, Douglas hoped, the roadways would be extended to link British Columbia with eastern Canada. "Who can foresee what the next ten years may bring forth," he wrote in 1863. "An overland Telegraph, *surely*, and a Railroad on British Territory, *probably*, the whole way from the Gulf of Georgia to the Atlantic." It was a long time coming, but Douglas was the first politician to champion the building of a national railway and highway.

Mifflin Wistar Gibbs, one of the free blacks who arrived from San Francisco, established a profitable general store, developed a coal mine, founded the first railway in the Queen Charlotte Islands (Haida Gwaii), organized the colony's first all-black militia—the African Rifles—then entered politics. In September 1868 he was Salt Spring Island's elected delegate to the Yale Convention, along with other pro-Confederation supporters like Amor De Cosmos (Victoria) and John Robson (New Westminster). The goal of the convention was to set the conditions for a speedy union of the Colony of

BC with the Dominion of Canada. With the gold rush now over, the colonial government was struggling with high debt levels as well as growing discontent among its ten thousand residents. Joining with Canada would be a solution to the colony's predicament.

The British Colonial Office in London saw strategic value in uniting British Columbia with Canada, but a major impediment lay in the three million hectares of HBC-owned lands (also known as Rupert's Land and the North-West Territory) separating the two entities. A solution was eventually arrived at in the Rupert's Land Act of 1868, by which the Canadian government agreed to purchase the territory from HBC for $1.5 million (£300,000). Soon after the transfer, a group of BC legislators travelled to Ottawa to continue negotiations over the details of the union. Once there, the delegates were surprised to find themselves in agreement with Canada on many items, including the need for a permanent rail link to the west coast within ten years. The final terms for admission of the colony were put before the BC electorate in November 1870 and approved. The legislation was then passed by the House of Commons and Senate in Ottawa and received Royal Assent on May 16, 1871. On July 20 of that year, British Columbia entered Confederation. Bells pealed, crowds filled Victoria streets, and in Esquimalt Harbour the flagship *Zealous* celebrated with a twenty-one-gun salute. Now, about that railroad.

The terms for the proposed new railway were as follows:

Canada would begin railway construction within two years and finish it in ten years, by 1883. The railway would cross 3,200 kilometres of swamp, bog, river, prairie, and mountain. It would bring in settlers and immigrants to the West, speed up inland travel, improve communications, and move freight more easily to market. The huge project would be built in a two-pronged attack. Construction crews would work from both the east and the west and meet in the middle at a point in the heights of the Rocky Mountains.

The need was identified, and the will was there, but from the start the project was beset with challenges. How would the young new nation of Canada muster the resources and expertise needed to execute such a massive project? Among the numerous problems to be solved was the puzzle of time zones—in particular, how to manage the scheduling of trains across such a vast distance. By the mid-nineteenth century, three types of time measurement were in use: natural time, local time, and railroad time. Time based on the natural movement of the sun across the sky was useful enough in agricultural areas, while local time, synchronized with astronomical measurements at the meridian of a specific location, was the time displayed on town clocks. Railroads kept time based on the city where the line started—Montreal, for example. Train travellers could synchronize their watches with local time, but any train schedule would be based on the time at the beginning location. England addressed this problem in 1847 by basing railway time on the meridian of the Royal Observatory at Greenwich. This was easy to do in a small country with only one time zone, but Canada was a different situation altogether.

Following a national bribery scandal in 1873 that unseated Macdonald's Conservative government, the new Liberal government of Alexander Mackenzie tackled the matter by establishing a new federal Department of Public Works and appointing Sandford Fleming, a respected surveyor and civil engineer, as engineer-in-chief of the preliminary coast-to-coast railway surveys. Fleming was considered a Renaissance man of many proven talents. As a surveyor and engineer for the Grand Trunk Railway Company, he had already designed the first Canadian postage stamp, the "three-penny beaver," issued in 1851. He used the beaver rather than British royalty to symbolize the nation's industrious habits, which he viewed as a Canadian characteristic. And Fleming knew all about railroad time. A contemporary of his, the American schoolteacher Charles Dowd, had proposed establishing Washington, DC, as the national meridian for a synchronized system of railroad time. Fleming took Dowd's idea to the next level, proposing an international standard that would divide the globe into twenty-four one-hour time zones beginning at Greenwich, England. In 1897, Queen Victoria knighted Fleming for his achievements, but it was not until 1929 that all major world countries accepted standardized time zones.

Under Fleming's leadership, the Canadian Pacific Survey was established and a survey party dispatched in 1872 to determine the ideal route for a transcontinental railway. The group would cross the rugged terrain of the Canadian Shield north of Lake Superior and work its way westward to the Rockies, where Fleming identified Yellowhead Pass as the most practicable route to British Columbia and the Pacific coast.

The Fleming party travelled some four thousand kilometres over eight years and played an important role in the exploration of Canada, but by the end of the 1870s, the political winds were changing again. The huge railway project was far behind schedule and in danger of collapse. De Cosmos, the pro-Confederation representative from BC, rose in the House of Commons to announce that any more delays would force BC into the open arms of the Americans. Influential businessmen in central Canada were lobbying for direct access to the raw materials and potential markets of the West. The howls for action finally brought about results. In the election of October 1880, Macdonald's Conservatives were restored to power. As one of its first actions, the new government decided to turn the management of the project over to a private company, and the Canadian Pacific Railway Company (CPR) was incorporated on February 16, 1881. George Stephen (later 1st Baron Mount Stephen) was its first president. Together with his cousin, Donald Smith, and associates James J. Hill and Richard B. Angus, Stephen was part of a consortium that had purchased the Saint Paul, Minneapolis, and Manitoba Railway in 1873.

The new private syndicate struck a contract with the Government of Canada to construct the trans-Canada railroad in exchange for $25 million in credit from the government and a land grant of 100,000 square kilometres, along with tax concessions and rights-of-way. The government also transferred to the new company those sections of the railway it had already constructed, defrayed surveying costs, and exempted the railway from property taxes for twenty years. It also placed a twenty-year prohibition on the construction of competing lines on the prairies that might provide feeder lines to US railways. Fleming was dismissed from his post as the new enterprise pressed ahead with the selection of private contractors to lay sections of track. But still, the obstacles were immense: political, financial, managerial, and, most important, logistical.

The town of Port Moody on Burrard Inlet was chosen for the western terminus of the rail line. All that remained was to get there. But the delays continued under the CPR, and during the 1881 construction season only 211 kilometres of track were completed. The chief engineer and general superintendent who had failed to put down more track were fired. The search was on for a leader who could get things moving.

William Cornelius Van Horne was an acclaimed American rail manager knowledgeable in every aspect of the industry. He could even drive a locomotive. Appreciating a challenge, and the generous salary of $15,000 a year, he agreed to leave Chicago to become general manager of the CPR, in charge of overseeing construction of the railway across the prairies and through the Rockies. A man who got to the point quickly in conversation, he believed railways should be built just as quickly. Van Horne claimed he could build eight hundred kilometres of main rail line in his first year, and, sure enough, despite severe flooding that delayed the start of the 1882 season out of Winnipeg, by year's end 673 kilometres of main line and 177 kilometres of branch line had been laid. The greatest engineering feat of its time was fast becoming reality.

While new to the West, train travel in eastern Canada had enjoyed a long tradition. Canada's first public train began running between Saint-Jean-sur-Richelieu and La Prairie near Montreal in 1836. By 1853, Grand Trunk trains were running between Montreal and Portland, Maine, a bustling commercial centre built around a year-round open harbour. In 1856, tracks were extended to join Montreal with Toronto and Sarnia, and by 1876 the 1,100-kilometre-long Intercolonial Railway was in place, connecting Ontario with Nova Scotia and New Brunswick. The addition of local rail lines like the Toronto, Grey and Bruce Railway to Georgian Bay in 1873 and the Toronto and Nipissing Railway to Lake Simcoe in 1877 would serve the rural hinterland. Next came the project of laying rail through the rugged Canadian Shield country north of Lake Superior. The route was needed so the eastern rail network could be joined to the new western route at Winnipeg, but along with the Rocky Mountain section, the north-of-Superior line would prove to be among the greatest challenges in the construction of the transcontinental railway.

CHAPTER

2

Eastward with Onderdonk

RAILROAD CONSTRUCTION WOULD START FROM both the east and the west and meet in the middle of the Rocky Mountains. In 1879, Andrew Onderdonk, a thirty-seven-year-old Dutch-American engineer who had just completed the San Francisco sea wall, was hired to build the western section of the trans-Canada railway through British Columbia. Over the next seven years, Onderdonk would lay 545 kilometres of track, from Port Moody to present-day Revelstoke, through some of the most formidable terrain in the country. Initially, the BC government contracted with multiple construction companies to lay different sections of the line, but Onderdonk's monetary muscle allowed him to buy out the other bidders with the rationale that work could be done faster and cheaper by one large company rather than many competing smaller ones.

Labour was in short supply, but Onderdonk managed to hire fifteen thousand "good, able-bodied, steady men" at $1.50 to $2.50 per day, prime wages at the time. He then charged them board at $4.50 per week. The work was labour-intensive and dangerous: clearing bush, blasting rock, moving debris, cutting through hills, unloading ties, and grading roadbed. Employee turnover was high. The back-breaking work was done by these "navvies" (a shortened version of the British term "navigator," applied to manual labourers on canal and railway civil engineering projects; Chinese labourers were called "coolies," a pejorative nickname for unskilled Asian workers). Table Mountain (Navvy Peak) near Golden, BC, pays homage to the CPR labourers and is now a site for alpine scrambling (a hybrid of extreme hiking and rock climbing) activities. On-the-job deaths were common. Those working in tunnels under construction were vulnerable to being crushed by roof collapses or blown to smithereens by explosions. Time was of the essence, and safety practices were minimal. Getting the job done was all that mattered.

Between 1881 and 1884, Onderdonk met his constant need for more workers by bringing in thousands of labourers from China and San Francisco. This was in direct violation of the BC government's racial policies to restrict the entry of Chinese into the province. Onderdonk argued

Chinese workers' camp, Kamloops, BC.
EDOUARD DEVILLE, LIBRARY AND ARCHIVES CANADA C-016715

that the labourers were needed if the project was to
succeed, prompting Prime Minister Macdonald to issue
an ultimatum to British Columbia: "Either you must have
this labour or you cannot have the railway." The Chinese
stayed, but they lived in separate areas and received only
one dollar a day, from which they had to pay for their food
(rice, dried salmon, and tea), tents, and cooking gear. Still,
these were high wages compared with the seven cents a day
they could earn back home, so any money they managed
to save would go a long way if they lived long enough to
return to China. Along with low pay, the Chinese got the

high-risk assignments—blasting tunnels through solid granite, hacking ledges out of steep cliffs, fording rapids by rope ladders, dangling from ropes to set charges. They suffered broken bones, crushed limbs, burns, infections, scurvy, sunstroke in summer, and frostbite in winter. Causes of death, if listed at all, included "crushed by a log," "killed by falling rock," "drowned," and "smothered by cave-in." Injuries and fatalities were so high, the hospital and cemetery at Yale, BC, were both full. Medical care was rudimentary for any worker on the rail line, but many Chinese relied on herbal treatments.

Unlike many of the self-made men who helped build the transcontinental railway, Onderdonk came from a refined, educated family and dressed more like a banker than a railway contractor. He, his wife, and their four children made Yale their home base during construction, where everyone from labourer to supervisor referred to him as "AO." During the first phase of construction, Onderdonk's men spent eighteen months blasting out four tunnels near Yale. Townspeople became resigned to the constant noise and shaking. The twenty-seven kilometres upriver from Yale required thirteen more tunnels to be cored out of the canyon granite.

All told, twenty-seven tunnels were built along the 340-kilometre stretch from Port Moody to Kamloops, along with some six hundred trestles and bridges. In one forty-eight-kilometre section alone, a hundred different structures were needed to span the vertical rock walls of multiple gorges and rivers. To build them, Onderdonk ordered forty million board feet of lumber, a board foot equalling the volume of a board that is one foot (30.5 centimetres) long, one foot wide, and one inch (2.5 centimetres) thick.

On the same trajectory as Onderdonk's railway was the old Cariboo Wagon Road built by James Douglas in the 1860s, which was still being used as a mining supply and stagecoach route. Now it was crowded by additional traffic from Onderdonk's supply line. Supplies were carried by yoked oxen and teams of up to twelve mules each pulling carts and wagons piled high with nails, rope, explosives, rations, and even movable sawmills, complete with pulleys, serrated blades, and hand cranks, so timber could be cut to fit on site. As well as sharing the twisting, cliff-hugging road, Onderdonk was obliged to maintain it for the public, since this was the only means of access to the Interior. Plus, he had to pay freight tolls. Frequently, traffic was halted for a percussive blast followed by rock cannonballing past terrified groups of animals and men. Sometimes a large chunk of the road was blown away by a miscalculated detonation and had to be rebuilt before rail tunnelling could continue. Every week workers were killed, but from dawn to dark it was rush hour on the precarious pathway with sheer rock on one side and a drop into oblivion on the other.

All this congestion and lost time were not the only costs. Onderdonk footed the bill for the mills and factories needed for the manufacture of explosives and building materials. He also paid for the charter ships used for fetching thousands of labourers from China. By mid-1882, already two years into the project, while the westward track was being laid rapidly across the prairies at a rate of five kilometres a day, Onderdonk had completed only thirty-two kilometres of rail in total. One kilometre of finished track was costing him an average of $128,000, vastly more than the cost of laying track across the flat prairie grassland. In desperation, he took to the water.

The narrow gorge on the Fraser River south of Boston Bar known as Hell's Gate was Onderdonk's nemesis. The narrows got its name in 1808 when explorer Simon Fraser saw the foaming water and wrote, "We had to travel where no human being should venture for surely we have encountered the gates of hell." Where high canyon walls squeeze the flow into a thirty-five-metre-wide chute, some 760 million litres of water rush through per minute—twice the volume of Niagara Falls.

At Hell's Gate, the men had to conduct their work suspended on ropes and ladders anchored to trees at the top of the cliffs. They dangled high over the foaming white water as they drilled blast holes and set charges into the wet rock face. Some of the navvies removed their boots to get better traction with their bare feet. The engineers had to make their measurements and cross-sections while suspended by ropes from the rim. One slip, frayed rope, loose rung, debris from above, or ill-timed explosion and they were dead, doomed to drop into the abyss, along with shredded trees and fractured boulders, as another section of rail tunnel or ledge was created.

Today, an aerial tram, suspension bridge, and observation tower at Hell's Gate provide a bird's-eye view over the precipice, but Onderdonk did not have that convenience. Instead, he had a sternwheeler built at Spuzzum that would carry supplies by water to the construction camps upstream. The sternwheeler, christened *Skuzzy*, was thirty-nine metres long by seven metres wide and had twenty watertight bulkheads for buoyancy. It would save him $10 per tonne in road tolls. On the day of its launch, crowds gathered along the water's edge to watch. Old-time river men bet against the ship getting through the Hell's Gate rapids. They were right. A second attempt was made. It too failed. Not to be defeated, Onderdonk had ringbolts for cables drilled into the canyon walls. Betting against success was now a hundred to one. But three months later, with 150 Chinese labourers on tow ropes pulling from the clifftop, the engines pounding, the steam winch turning, and more workers cranking the capstan, the S.S. *Skuzzy I* made it through Hell's Gate against the current and upstream to Lytton. There, for the next year, she worked as a river freighter supplying the construction of CPR tunnels, retaining walls, and bridges. After every journey she had to be patched up from hull damage caused by the bruising and bashing rapids and rocks. And every time, she went back into the water and did it all over again.

* * *

For every section laid, Onderdonk's crews were able to move materials forward by rail to the next work site. Onderdonk set up his own machine shop and foundry to build the rolling stock and purchased locomotives in the United States, which were brought to BC by boat. When an innovative bridge was needed to cross the Fraser River at Cisco (now called Siska) near Lytton, he hired the American civil engineer Charles Conrad Schneider to design it. The CPR was Schneider's first big client. The bridge he designed was one of the first cast iron and steel cantilever structures of the time. Today, with a second bridge on the opposite bank and the Trans-Canada Highway running parallel to both, photographers can frame two trains together on the two facing Cisco Bridges. Schneider went on to design the Stoney Creek Viaduct in the Selkirk Mountains. Though built of untreated wood as a temporary structure in 1885, the bridge would last until 1893, when it was replaced by a steel-arch bridge, also designed by C.C. Schneider.

By 1884, Onderdonk had completed the Fraser Canyon section of the rail and reached Savona's Ferry (now Sevona), near Kamloops. He was then contracted by the CPR to continue construction through Kamloops and present-day Revelstoke to Eagle Pass, on the western approach to the Rockies. He continued to use steamboats to supply his crews, which gave him an advantage compared with the situation faced by crews approaching from the east.

An Onderdonk crew at work on construction of the span over the Nicola River in the BC Interior, 1882. CANADIAN PACIFIC ARCHIVES NS-5273

But the construction challenges kept coming. Kamloops was one of those rare settlements that existed before the railway arrived, and surveys had placed the rail line right through the centre of town, essentially slicing the community in two. Then there was the livestock complication. Thousands of cattle on open range posed a danger to trains (and the cattle), so the line had to be fenced between Kamloops and Shuswap Lake. Next, six tunnels rimming the shore of Shuswap Lake had to be cored out of solid rock. Even Mother Nature seemed to be against the crews. The hot, dry summer of 1884 resulted in numerous forest fires near Kamloops. A stockpile of between five thousand and twelve thousand rail ties went up in flames. As a result, the section beginning at Notch Hill used only half the required number of ties. Instead of 1,875 ties per kilometre, here only 1,000 were used. This left the heavy 70-pound (31.8-kilogram) rails used for mountain construction, as opposed to the regular 56-pound (25.4-kilogram) ones used elsewhere, resting on fewer ties. Onderdonk also ran out of telegraph wire at Notch Hill. Sicamous was reached on September 15, 1885. Ten days later, on the west slope of Eagle Pass, he ran out of rails and discharged all his men. Thousands of navvies returned to Yale any way they could. Onderdonk had completed his allotted section of track, even if there were questions about the quality of construction and the lifespan of bridges and masonry. It was now up to crews from the east to join up the rail.

The British Columbia section of the CPR was completed by Onderdonk up to Eagle Pass, twenty kilometres west of Revelstoke, between 1880 and 1885, through a series of five government contracts plus one contract with the CPR. These included Contract 60 from Emory's Bar to Boston Bar (46 kilometres) for $2,727,300; Contract 61 from Boston Bar to Lytton (46 kilometres) for $2,573,640; Contract 62 from Lytton to Junction Flat (45 kilometres) for $2,056,950; Contract 63 from Junction Flat to Savona's Ferry (65 kilometres) for $1,746,150; Contract 92 (part) from Emory's Bar to Port Moody (138 kilometres) for $178,981; and the CPR contract from Savona's Ferry to Eagle Pass (274 kilometres). The complete route included 644 kilometres of main line, with 341 kilometres of that following the canyon terrain of the Fraser and Thompson Rivers. Approximately fifteen thousand men were employed on the Onderdonk contracts, more than half of them labourers from China.

Onderdonk is recognized for building one of the most difficult sections of the transcontinental railway; however, several sections of the line were of substandard quality. CPR manager Van Horne stated that the truss bridges were "the worst I ever saw in a railway" and applied for public funding to bring all the track up to an acceptable level. J.H. Pope, minister of railways and canals for the federal government, at first refused and insisted the line be used as it was. But multiple landslides, washouts, and bridge failures eventually forced the government (a.k.a. taxpayers) to reimburse the CPR for retrofit work on the wildest sections of line.

3

Passages West

WHILE ANDREW ONDERDONK WAS CONSTRUCTING the rail line east through British Columbia, CPR crews had worked their way across the prairies to the eastern slope of the Rockies. Their next task was to find a way through the seemingly impenetrable mountain ranges. The pressure was intense. If no workable route could be found, the entire transcontinental railway project would be a colossal failure. Fortunately, previous expeditions and surveyors had mapped out multiple possibilities from which a final route could be assembled. But "getting through" was as much an act of faith as of exploration and taming the wilderness. Many possible routes were discovered and tested, but right up to the end there was no clear plan for which one they would choose and how they would engineer their way through.

The North American Cordillera is the geological name for the extensive mountain chain running along the western side of North America from Alaska to the southern border of Mexico. In Canada, the southernmost point is at the US border, while the northernmost point is in northern British Columbia. It includes consecutive north-south ranges beginning east of the Alberta–British Columbia border: the Rocky, Purcell, Selkirk, Monashee, Cascade, and Coast Mountains. These six ranges, with their plateaus, canyons, alpine lakes, rivers, and glaciers, occupy much of the territory west of the Prairies. They also contain some of the highest peaks in North America, including Mount Robson at 3,954 metres and Mount Columbia at 3,747 metres.

It was through this formidable series of barriers that the Canadian Pacific Railway intended to lay its tracks. The Pacific Survey faced two problems: the selection of a western rail terminus, and engineering a route from the east side of the Rockies through to the west side. It took ten years of surveying during the 1870s and 1880s to find the cheapest, most direct route. Like the establishment of trading posts during the fur trade, whatever route was finally chosen would affect the development of the country for decades to come. Towns near the rail line would prosper and grow. Bypassed settlements would wither and die. The CPR line controlled their fate.

In 1880, the preferred route staked out by Sandford Fleming was across the parkland of the northern prairies and through the Rockies via Yellowhead Pass (named for Pierre Bostonais, nicknamed Tête Jaune, an Iroquois/European guide in the 1820s with a yellow streak in his hair), to the west of Edmonton. At only 1,110 metres high, Yellowhead is the lowest crossing of the Continental Divide in all of North America. Fleming was fired when Macdonald's federal government assigned the railway project to the newly formed CPR, but his efforts were not in vain. While Yellowhead was not the route finally selected for the CPR, it was later used by the Canadian Northern Railway (later merged with Canadian National Railway as CN) and Grand Trunk Pacific Railway. Later still, the pass was used as a major highway crossing through the Rocky Mountains.

Well before Fleming, earlier survey parties had scouted various sections of the Cordillera, each of them contributing pieces of the puzzle that would eventually point to a viable route for rail passage through the high peaks. In the 1850s, members of the Palliser Expedition travelled west by steamer, canoe, wagon, and horseback and on foot. Where the country was too rough for pack animals, men did the packing. Multiple armies of surveyors spread out across the mountains, where they lived in tents, cooked on open fires, pushed through dense bush, and scrambled over rough terrain. They carried firearms for protection and for foraging for fresh game while fighting frostbite, scurvy, mosquitoes, bears, wolves, fleas, forest fires, and the constant threat of death by drowning in raging rivers. While some loved the freedom of this outdoor life, others found the isolation and separation from family an additional hardship. Surveyors packed their own provisions and surveying instruments, including compasses, scopes, theodolites, and transits to measure the angles between landmarks, plus field books and pocket slates for noting observations and measurements. They used thirty-metre survey chains to measure length. They followed existing maps to the extent of their geographical information, then began filling in the blanks. This was the objective of an adventurer from abroad who saw the western lands as open for discovery and in need of scientific analysis.

* * *

John Palliser, a young Irish sportsman, enjoyed his first North American hunting expedition in 1847 so much that he wrote about his adventures and asked the Royal Geographical Society in London to fund a return trip. It in turn petitioned the British government, which needed the HBC territories (Rupert's Land) surveyed for land claims and possibly a railroad. American survey expeditions were crossing into British North America territory, so, wishing to maintain their claim to the West, Britain funded Palliser's proposal with a grant of £5,000. The Palliser Expedition (1857–60) was a first. Specifically, they were mandated to explore the old North West Company canoe route west from Lake Superior, the plains of the South and North Saskatchewan Rivers, and the routes through the southern Rockies to the Pacific coast.

In the summer of 1857, the Palliser group left Lower Fort Garry (now Winnipeg) with carts, wagons, men, and horses and proceeded to move along unmarked American prairie border lands. They overwintered at Fort Carlton on the North Saskatchewan River. Throughout their journey they gathered scientific information, including astronomical, meteorological, geological, and magnetic data. They recorded detailed descriptions of the landscape, flora, fauna, and First Nations customs and made recommendations on the potential for settlement and transportation. The main team consisted of Palliser, skilled in wilderness survival, as leader; Dr. James Hector, a geologist, naturalist, and surgeon; Eugène Bourgeau, a botanical collector; John W. Sullivan, secretary and astronomical observer; and Lieutenant Thomas W. Blakiston, magnetic observer. While the men were members of the same expedition, they often fanned out individually to cover more territory. Dr. Hector frequently travelled in advance of the others to check out the terrain and hire local Native guides.

The Palliser Expedition explored six of the Rocky Mountain passes: Howse, North Kananaskis, North Kootenay, South Kootenay, and two discovered by James Hector himself—Vermilion and Kicking Horse. The Palliser group also explored the Cypress Hills and Kootenay River and followed the Columbia River to Fort Vancouver in Washington State before returning home to England. Its extensive three-volume report, including detailed maps, was published in 1859, 1860, and 1865. By then the US was consumed by the American Civil War, and western expansion into Rupert's Land was not a high priority for them.

When James Hector reached Vermilion Pass in 1858, a mountain pass that crosses the Continental Divide at 1,661 metres, he wrote in his journal that they had finally reached "the first water we had seen flowing to the Pacific." The pass, which he named for the reddish-brown (ochre) clay used by First Nations to make pigments, today connects Banff National Park in Alberta with Kootenay National Park in British Columbia. Highway 93 travels through as it connects Castle Mountain with Radium Hot Springs. But a second pass discovered along the Kicking Horse River was prob-lematic. The valley of the Kicking Horse River was seldom used by local First Nations, who considered it too wild and dangerous for their horses. As Hector's small party picked its way through the underbrush, one of the pack horses stumbled and, in an attempt to break free, plunged into the river. Hector later recorded the incident, writing that "the banks were so steep that we had great difficulty in getting him out. In attempting to re-catch my own horse, which had strayed off while we were engaged with the one in the water, he kicked me in the chest, but I had luckily got close to him before he struck out, so that I did not get the full force of the blow." But it did land with a significant thud that flattened Hector to the ground and broke his ribs. His guide, Peter Erasmus, later recalled, "We all leapt from our horses and rushed up to him, but all our attempts to help him recover his senses were of no avail . . . Dr. Hector must have been unconscious for at least two hours when Sutherland yelled for us to come up; he was now conscious but in great pain. He asked for his kit and directed me to prepare some medicine that would ease the pain."

Until that point, the men were convinced their leader was dead—so convinced, in fact, that they dug his grave. He had not recovered his ability to speak, and had it not been for Hector blinking his eyes, they might have buried him alive. Still in pain, he managed to remount, and the party carried on. Food was scarce, and the men were reduced to scavenging for roots and eating wild berries until a lucky shot brought down a grouse at Wapta Lake, near the summit of a pass on the Continental Divide. They camped there and "were happy to boil it up with some ends of candles and odd pieces of grease, to make something like a supper for the five of us after a very hard day's work." The next day a moose was shot, and with the additional protein, the men began to regain their strength. While Mount Hector and Hector Lake were named for James Hector, his men thought it appropriate to name the river in honour of the kicking-horse incident, and the pass above was assigned the same name.

During the same period as Palliser, other travellers were exploring routes west and making significant contributions to mapping the little-known territory through the Rockies. Between 1859 and 1863, a group of 150 settlers known as the Overlanders set out in two bands from eastern Canada in search of a better life in the Cariboo goldfields. Compared with the average farming wage of two dollars a day, miners could make several hundred dollars a day panning for gold. Most potential prospectors arrived in BC by sea, but the Overlanders were remarkable for making the journey by land. In June 1862, a large party left Fort Garry (Winnipeg) with Red River carts, oxen, and horses, reaching Fort Edmonton in July, where they restocked and prepared to cross the Rockies. They decided to head for Yellowhead Pass, recommended by some returning miners. The Overlanders straggled across the land in a long line. The first members of the party crossed through the pass but were facing hunger. Subsisting on squirrels and small birds, they had to slaughter some of their oxen and horses for food. They reached the Shuswap salmon-fishing camp at Tête Jaune Cache in late August, where they traded ammunition, clothing, needles, and thread for fish, saskatoon berries, and pemmican. A second group made it through the pass, but when they stopped at Yellowhead Lake, they became stranded by rising waters. Rescued by the third, and last, party of Overlanders, they continued their westbound trek together.

Having survived the harrowing passage through the

Rockies, the reunited Overlanders decided to split up again and take different routes to the Cariboo. The larger group opted for following the Fraser River to Fort George (Prince George), then south to Quesnel. For transportation, they hollowed out cottonwood logs to make canoes covered with ox hide. The first part of the journey went well, but at Scow Rapids some of the canoes capsized, and four men drowned. The remaining travellers reached their destination in October 1862. The smaller group decided to travel overland along the McLennan River north to the Fraser. Imagining the long land trek ahead of them, they purchased one hundred head of livestock, only to discover that the route would require downstream travel along the Thompson River. The cattle were slaughtered, the horses turned loose, and rafts constructed for the water journey. At Murchison Rapids they ran into trouble, and two men drowned. Finally, the survivors arrived at Thompson's River Post (Kamloops), also in October 1862. The only female Overlander, Catherine O'Hare Schubert, was in this group, along with her husband, Augustus, and their three children. A day after arriving at their destination, she gave birth to their fourth child, a daughter called Rose, the first white girl to be born in the British Columbia Interior. Few Overlanders ended up working the goldfields, but their passage through the Rockies demonstrated that topography was not destiny and geographical impediments to union between eastern Canada and BC were not insurmountable.

* * *

Walter Moberly, a surveyor and civil engineer, was working as assistant surveyor general for the Colony of British Columbia in 1864 when he too became involved in the search for a passable route through the Rockies. Part of Moberly's role was to survey new travel routes for the region's growing population. Busy with official survey work, he realized he would not have time to personally scout out the Illecillewaet River, a tributary of the Columbia River that passes through the Selkirk Mountains at what is now known as Rogers Pass, so he sent his assistant, Albert Perry. Perry returned a month later with the news that no mountain pass existed. Moberly was disappointed, then furious when he discovered that Perry had not gone all the way through a narrow gap up Connaught Creek. The following year, Moberly found a route through the adjacent Monashee Mountains, which he named Eagle Pass, then pushed farther east up the Illecillewaet River in the Selkirks. He envisioned an overland railway coming through Howse Pass, across the Great Divide, around the Big Bend, and through Eagle Pass. He just had to discover the precise route.

A few years later, as the Canadian railway project was getting underway, Sandford Fleming believed Moberly's mountain experience and knowledge of the backcountry made him the obvious choice to lead all exploratory and location surveys for the CPR in BC. Fleming gave him the go-ahead to hire men for his survey parties. Moberly set his sights on Howse Pass (1,539 metres). Located in present-day Banff National Park, Howse Pass links the North Saskatchewan and Columbia River systems. It was used by the Ktunaxa (Kootenay) people to reach buffalo herds on the plains. The pass was first surveyed in 1807 by David Thompson, a North West Company explorer and fur trader. In 1809, it was named for Joseph Howse, a Hudson's Bay Company employee. For a time, it was considered the preferred route by the CPR. However, in 1872 Moberly was ordered to cease work on Howse and take all his men to Yellowhead to work on Fleming's preferred choice. Moberly declined to follow these orders, choosing instead to continue working on his favoured route, and on February 13, 1873, he was relieved of his duties. He was replaced by Marcus Smith, an engineer who had worked on the Intercolonial Railway in eastern Canada and went on to serve as the chief CPR engineer in British Columbia. Moberly moved on to work in California, then returned to Winnipeg in 1875, where, among other projects, he designed the city's first sewer system before returning to Vancouver in 1898 for some northern railway assignments.

Marcus Smith had a formidable job ahead of him. Among other responsibilities, he was tasked with finding a Pacific deep-sea port terminus for the railroad. In the 1870s, the BC inland wilderness was *terra incognita* to most of the financiers, managers, civil engineers, and surveyors of the CPR. But it was essential that they find a route to link up the

Interior Plateau with a deep-water Pacific port. As Fleming's man in charge, Smith explored possible options from Port Simpson in the north to Burrard Inlet in the south. Some of the sites considered included Bute Inlet on the Homathco River, Dean Channel on the Kimsquit River, Gardner Canal on the Kitlope River, Kemano on the Kitimat River, and the Skeena River area. Smith eventually settled on Bute Inlet as his preferred western rail terminus, but Burrard Inlet was preferred by railroad management.

John Macoun, a Canadian naturalist, accompanied the Fleming survey party to the Pacific in 1872 to assess the agricultural potential of the West. Macoun believed the southerly Kicking Horse Pass should be used by the railroad in order to serve the more fertile lands of present-day southern Alberta and provide a more direct route to American markets. However, Macoun's visit corresponded with a year of high rainfall, giving the usually arid semi-desert region the appearance of being lush and green. Still, the government and railroad governors agreed with him. As more and more information favouring a southern passage accumulated, Fleming's choice of the Yellowhead Pass lost support and was abandoned in 1881.

All focus now turned to the possibility of a route through Kicking Horse Pass and the Illecillewaet Valley, an option foreseen by Moberly back in 1865. It would shorten the length of the western line but present a significant engineering obstacle with two mountain ranges to get through, the

Rockies and the Selkirks. So, more than fifteen years after the first survey by Moberly and Perry, Sandford Fleming travelled through the Illecillewaet Valley on the western slope of the Rockies and described his party's hardships: "The walking is dreadful, we climb over and creep under fallen trees of great size and the men soon show that they feel the weight of their burdens. Their halts for rest are frequent. It is hot work for us all. The dripping rain from the bush and branches saturates us from above. Tall ferns sometimes reaching to the shoulder and Devil's Clubs ... may be numbered by millions and they are perpetually wounding us with their spikes against which we strike. Our advance is varied by ascending rocky slopes and slippery masses, and again descending to a lower level. We wade through Alder swamps and tread down Skunk Cabbage and Prickly Aralias, and so we continue until half-past four, when the tired-out men are able to go no further." Fleming's official survey report would quote both Moberly's 1871 journal entry, which states, "I found there was not any practicable pass through the Selkirk range," and Marcus Smith's finding that "there is little probability of a pass being found across the Selkirk range between the upper and lower arms of the Columbia River."

Edouard Gaston Deville also worked on the survey of the newly acquired North-West Territories for the Dominion of Canada. In 1880, he joined the federal government's homestead survey for settlement of the prairies with the

Department of the Interior. In 1881, he was appointed inspector for Dominion Land Surveys and in 1885 became surveyor general. Deville developed innovative methods of tackling surveying challenges in the Rockies. He expanded on French army engineer Aimé Laussedat's principle of elevated photography and refined the process of creating large-scale maps from photographs, a technique known as photogammetry. Deville also designed a rugged, lightweight field camera that could be carried long distances and, from 1888 to 1896, created some of the most accurate maps to date of the Rocky Mountain terrain. Mount Deville in Yoho National Park is named in his honour, and a commemorative plaque is located near the entrance to the park's Monarch Campground.

* * *

The plethora of Rocky Mountain expeditions and surveys in the 1800s generated a wealth of information but did not make choosing the final route through the mountains any easier. There was no one formula to balance the different factors. Fleming held that the ideal route would include such engineering features as "low gradients, easy alignments, and permanently firm roadbed, at the least annual capital outlay . . . capable of transporting cheaply." His second-tier transit considerations were "local resources, through traffic, and terminus (location) that determine returns after completion." For Marcus Smith, "the particular duty of an engineer is to get the physical features of the country, to ascertain them and exhibit them by maps and profiles so as to form an idea from which he can get the quantities to form an estimate of the cost of constructing a railway across the country." Smith added that "in exploring, [the engineer] is expected to get all the information he can as to the soil . . . timber, produce. They all have a certain bearing on the location. It sometimes would be advisable to construct a line that would cost a good deal more on account of the country having more resources."

But the precise route through the Selkirks had still not been found, even though tracks were now being laid at a furious pace directly toward the southern route. Gambling that a pass would be found, the Canadian Pacific syndicate made the ultimate corporate decision to build its eastern approach directly across the prairies to the difficult Kicking Horse Pass. It would be an expensive gamble if it failed, and shaky finances were as much of a challenge to the transcontinental rail project as soaring geography.

In February 1881, a man was found for the job of punching a route into the mountains. Albert Bowman (A.B.) "Hell's Bells" Rogers was a short, scrawny 52-year-old with flaring whiskers, a foul mouth, and a fascination with immortality. He was an American engineer who had served as a major in the US cavalry during the Dakota Sioux uprising in 1862. He later earned a reputation as the "railway pathfinder" for his engineering location work across the American Midwest. A plains surveyor, Rogers had "never seen a mountain," but he was the one man up to pushing through the vertical escarpments, massive glaciers, and dark forests of the Selkirk range. When describing the "engineering saviour" of the CPR, William Van Horne once commented that Rogers was "somewhat eccentric and given to 'burning brimstone,'" but was a "very good man on construction, honest and fair dealing."

Rogers drove his men hard, fed them miserly rations, and cursed them regularly. Few stayed around very long. He was equally demanding of himself, though. He was parsimonious with his employer's money and kept crew expenses to a minimum. He travelled with a compass, scruffy overalls, chewing tobacco, and hardtack biscuits. His surveyors joked that this was an entire year's food for "the old man."

Rogers's assignment was to lay out the shortest route between the city of Regina and Andrew Onderdonk's end-of-line in British Columbia. While the Rockies were known to have Howse, Yellowhead, Kicking Horse, Kootenay, and Vermilion Passes, the Selkirks were a mystery. If Rogers solved that mystery and found a way through, the CPR would pay him $5,000 and name the pass in his honour. The money was good, but having his name immortalized forever on a high-profile geographic feature was irresistible. Rogers began by reviewing all previous survey reports, including those of Moberly. He was so confident about finding a pass that a line toward the Selkirks was surveyed right up the Bow River Valley and over the Continental Divide via Kicking Horse Pass.

Earlier in 1881, while hastily completing survey work for the prairie section of the CPR, Rogers had assumed that the simplest rail route west would be through the Bow River Valley. Faced with steep cliffs and treacherous river crossings in the approach to Mount Rundle near Banff, his survey team recommended bypassing the peak with a 275-metre-long tunnel through an adjacent peak to be called Tunnel Mountain. Van Horne was incensed when he heard the suggestion, shouting, "Are we going to hold up this railway for a year and a half while they build their damned tunnel? Take it out!" The tunnel idea was immediately dropped, and an alternative route to the north was located. One of the surveyors, Charles Shaw, described the proposal as "the most extraordinary engineering blunder I have ever known in the way of engineering." While the tunnel concept was scrapped altogether, that mountain in Banff National Park is still called Tunnel Mountain to this day.

By June 1881, Rogers and his party, approaching from the west, had struggled all the way up the Illecillewaet Valley beyond where Albert Perry had turned back fifteen years earlier. At the headwaters, he thought he saw a way through at the pinnacle (a point later named Mount Sir Donald in

Major Albert B. Rogers.
GLENBOW ARCHIVES NA-1949-1

Andrew Onderdonk.
TOPLEY STUDIO, LIBRARY AND ARCHIVES
CANADA E008300902

Captain John Palliser and
Dr. James Hector.
GLENBOW ARCHIVES NA-588-1

CPR president William C.
Van Horne.
LIBRARY AND ARCHIVES CANADA C-008549

54

honour of CPR director Donald A. Smith), but his stingy management of rations came back to haunt him. The crews were out of supplies. If they did not turn back immediately to the Columbia River, he and his men would not make it. So, only twenty-nine kilometres away from success, he turned around. However, in anticipation of eventual success, Rogers did report that a pass existed.

The following May, he made a second attempt, this time starting from the east via Beaver River where it joins the Columbia River. Again he ran out of supplies and had to retreat and resupply. He tried again, following the Beaver, then its tributary, the Bear River. The third try was the charm. On July 24, 1882, Rogers reached the opening through the peaks that would forever bear his name. He received his cheque from the CPR but refused to cash it, preferring instead to have it framed and hung on the wall, because, after all, he had not done it for the money. It took the intervention of Van Horne, who presented Rogers with an elaborately decorated gold watch, before he would cash the cheque and the accountants could balance the books. The CPR had its route through the mountains.

4

Kootenay Connections

THE CPR HAD FOUND ITS PATH WEST, winding upward from the Alberta plains to the high peaks of the Kicking Horse and Rogers Passes and down again to Revelstoke, BC, where it would link with the transcontinental route to the coast. In the following decades, new regional lines would be added to serve the growing agricultural and mining economies of southern BC and Alberta, bringing new engineering challenges.

The first of these was the Crowsnest Pass line. Not part of the initial CPR advance, the pass was first surveyed in 1892, tracing a route from Lethbridge, Alberta, along the north side of the Oldman River to Kootenay Landing, near Nelson, BC. In 1897–98 the new line was built. Crossing

Crowsnest Pass at an elevation of 1,358 metres, it is the most southerly rail and highway route through the Canadian Rockies and the lowest mountain pass in Canada south of the Yellowhead. The Crowsnest line had a strategic purpose, which was to assert Canadian sovereignty (not to mention CPR economic dominance) against US railroad incursions into the region. But it also opened access to the area's newly discovered coal and mineral deposits in BC's Elk River Valley, providing the means for the CPR to convert its steam locomotives from wood to coal power.

The CPR sought and received financial assistance for the Crowsnest line from the federal government, partially in exchange for a freight subsidy on prairie farm exports and equipment imports. The Crow Rate, as the agreement was called, eventually applied to all railway lines in western Canada, regardless of corporate ownership or location. This created artificially low freight rates for wheat shipments to the world through Great Lakes ports. The subsidy also limited industrial growth in the west, since it was cheaper to manufacture items in the east and ship them west under the Crow Rate. The subsidy was finally abolished in 1995. Today, Highway 3 and an oil pipeline run through the pass parallel to the rail line.

Construction of the Kettle Valley Railway (KVR), also known as the Coast-to-Kootenay connection, started in 1910 to connect the farm, lumber, and mining industries along the British Columbia–US border to the CPR mainline. It was a local "milk run," servicing small communities in stunning landscapes. From Midway in the West Kootenay region, the Kettle Valley Railway passed through the mining centres of Beaverdell and Carmi and crossed over the Okanagan Highlands via the Monashee Mountains to Penticton in the Okanagan Valley, then beyond, over Trout Creek Canyon, to West Summerland. It crossed the Interior Plateau of the Cascade Mountains to Princeton and Coalmount in the Tulameen Valley, then ascended back into the Cascades to Brodie Junction. There the rail line branched in two directions. To the north, it followed the Coldwater River Valley to Merritt, where it joined an existing CPR branch line (the Nicola branch) leading westward to the CPR mainline at Spences Bridge in the Thompson River Valley. To the south, it travelled along the Coquihalla River Valley, through the narrow Coquihalla Pass in the Hope Mountains, and connected with the CPR mainline at Odlum in the lower Fraser River Valley near Hope.

The KVR ran for 525 kilometres and was headquartered at Penticton in the Okanagan Valley. As a wholly owned subsidiary of the CPR, the KVR operated as a secondary line, often called upon when washouts, avalanches, and rock slides shut the main CPR line through the Fraser Canyon. It was absorbed into the CPR in 1937 as the Kettle Valley Division. The CPR wanted to block an incursion by its rival, Great Northern, which ran from Saint Paul, Minnesota, to Seattle, Washington, giving it easy access to southern BC from low valleys in Washington State.

Andrew McCulloch accepted the job of chief engineer for the construction of the Kettle Valley Railway on the understanding that, as directed by the BC government and the CPR, the KVR "must be first class in every way." But from the start, McCulloch faced problems in securing locomotives, materials, and workers. Two years into the work, only 20 percent of the line was complete. The next year, to speed up construction, over five thousand men were hired as KVR navvies, and the project, "one of the strangest railways ever built," was completed within five years. The proud CPR president Thomas Shaughnessy travelled the entire route from Midway to Hope on September 14, 1916. Throngs of excited residents lined the tracks in every town along the way because their long-promised Coast-to-Kootenay connection was finally a reality. The railway provided not only a faster and more efficient route for Okanagan fruit going to market but also carried ore and lumber, men in search of jobs, and students heading for university.

Andrew McCulloch had overcome formidable challenges and used amazing construction techniques in building this railway marvel. The Kettle Valley Railway included forty-three bridges, requiring twenty-two million board feet of lumber and 4,500 tonnes of steel; thirteen tunnels; and sixteen snowsheds. Hanging precariously from canyon walls and dangling by ropes, McCulloch surveyed the area personally and developed a plan for a series of tunnels. Using perfectly aligned tunnels with two bridges between three of them, he managed to build a route across Myra Canyon. The Kettle Valley Railway was impressive, indeed, but proved to be a challenging railway to maintain, with rock, mud, and snow slides constantly damaging the rail line. Today, the railway has been taken out and replaced with a foot bridge to allow tourists to view McCulloch's civil engineering marvel.

The Myra Canyon trestles near Kelowna in the Okanagan Valley were McCulloch's masterpiece. In an outstanding feat of engineering, he placed supporting structures near the canyon rim, thousands of metres above the trees and creeks below, and cut track bed into the sloping rock walls. The railway entered the canyon just west of Myra Station, then was sculpted to the contours of the U-shaped canyon's walls and across two chasms at East Canyon and West Canyon, where Pooley Creek had cleft huge ravines. The line was almost level throughout the canyon, with only a 0.40 percent upward grade from Myra Station to the summit at Mile 85.9, at an elevation of 1,274 metres, then a slight 0.40 percent downward grade running west from the summit. Within a distance of ten kilometres, twenty wooden trestles were assembled to carry the rail line over wide spaces and deep depressions in the canyon walls. To make things even more interesting, all were built on curves arcing seven to twelve degrees to conform to the natural contours of the canyon. This minimized the amount of excavating needed along sections between the trestles. One trestle at Mile 87.4 was built in an S shape, with

The route of the Kettle Valley Railway. Constructed between 1910 and 1915, the KVR provided regional train service to the mining and farm communities of southern British Columbia.

a twelve-degree right turn followed by a twelve-degree left turn to fit along the winding canyon wall from east to west. Line curvature was minimized by designing sweeping curves across multiple trestles and turning the line gradually along the length of longer trestles. The largest of the wooden frame trestles at Mile 87.9, crossing West Fork Canyon Creek, was a breathtaking 229 metres long and 55 metres high, turning the rail almost ninety degrees over its entire length while not exceeding a curvature of twelve degrees anywhere along its length. Some observers claimed that the whole rail line

61

through Myra Canyon seemed to be one continuous line of trestles. Although not the largest trestles ever constructed on a Canadian railway, the placement, configuration, number, and alignments of the Myra Canyon trestles were unmatched by any other ten-kilometre section of Canadian railway.

Overall, the construction and positioning of the Myra Canyon trestles greatly reduced the amount of rock excavation needed to build the rail bed through the canyon, with only two tunnels and three deep rock cuts required to complete the section. These were built by hand on either curves or tangents to curves to align with the line's winding path along the canyon walls. But that is not to minimize the tunnels' impressive size. The East Tunnel at Mile 85.7 was 114 metres long on a twelve-degree curve; the West Tunnel at Mile 86.4 was 85 metres long on a seven-degree curve; and the rock cuts at Mile 84.7 and Mile 86.7 were 9 to 12 metres deep and bisected solid rock outcroppings on the canyon walls. All were left in their natural state post-construction, as if they had just been blasted out of the rock. Any loose rock was removed by hand scaling, but the natural look prevailed. No sooner was the rail line open than the structures clinging to the mountainside in Myra Canyon were recognized as phenomenal feats of railway engineering. The public, and even McCulloch's assistant engineers, nicknamed the Kettle Valley Railway "McCulloch's Wonder."

Another impressive feat from this period was the construction of the tunnels through the ninety-one-metre-deep

Coquihalla Gorge. These were built using the help of only black powder, hand tools, and horse-drawn scrapers. A straight line of five tunnels, known as the Othello or Quintette Tunnels, was drilled east of Hope. The first tunnel is the largest, and there are viewing spaces between tunnels where the Coquihalla River can be seen far below. McCullough, an avid Shakespeare buff, used character names such as Lear, Jessica, Portia, Iago, Romeo, and Juliet to name stations in what is now the Coquihalla Canyon Provincial Park. This section of rail was one of the most expensive stretches of railway track in the world to construct, costing approximately $300,000 in 1914, equal to $5.8 million today.

In 1905, Midway, BC, was the site of a knock-down, drag-'em-out barroom brawl between construction workers for the CPR and its rival, the Great Northern Railway. The two companies were in constant competition over which of them would have the right to lay track through Kettle Valley. The railway navvies held no personal grudges, but they were tough, rowdy men, and the prospect of a good free-for-all broke the monotony of spiking down rails day after day. Besides, the winning side got bragging rights until its next encounter. Fortunately, this altercation, fuelled by the consumption of multiple fermented beverages, took place on the Canadian side of the border, where personal firearms were not allowed. The men used fists, axe handles, and furniture instead of guns. Still, these handy weapons resulted in broken bones and severe bruises.

The first day of fighting ended in a draw. Each side retreated and called for reinforcements. Fearing a full-scale battle scene the next day, Midway officials had all the bars closed and the liquor locked down. Next morning, looking for both refreshment and a rematch, CPR workers crossed the nearby border to saloons in Ferry, Washington, where they crashed a street party of their GNR rivals. Given the choice of resuming combat or joining in the carousing, they decided to make merry this time and fight another day. Each of the competing railways launched lawsuits that cost them enough in legal fees to build nineteen kilometres of track. Who won the battle of Midway, BC? The lawyers!

When the KVR first started operations, its locomotives burned coal from Coalmont, BC, a small mining town northwest of Princeton. It was top-quality coal and worked well in steam locomotives, making the engine firemen very happy. The coal's superior burning features meant they had to shovel less of it into the firebox during their long twelve-hour shifts to maintain power through the steep Cascade Mountains. Their preference was confirmed in 1931 when an industry report stated that the Coalmont vein was one of two top deposits of locomotive coal in North America. In response, Coalmont raised its prices. The CPR, which had operational control of KVR, immediately switched to a less expensive fuel supplier, a mine in Merritt, BC. Firemen now had to work harder. They retaliated by saying they were employed by CHEA-P-R.

Wonder that it was, the KVR died the death of a thousand cuts. In 1949, the Hope-Princeton section of Highway 3 opened. The KVR Copper Mountain branch was abandoned in 1957 when the mine closed, and KVR lost more of its prominence when the Crowsnest Highway was built. Finally, in November 1959, heavy rains washed out sections of the line that were never repaired. With annual snowfalls above four metres, avalanches, rock slides, and forest fires, the KVR was no longer viable as a rail line. After the closure, rail traffic was routed to Spences Bridge and Merritt in order to maintain the connection with the remainder of the line. Through freight was discontinued in 1962 and passenger traffic in 1964. All rail service was halted from Midway to Penticton (including the famed Myra Canyon section) in 1973 and all track declared abandoned in 1978. Rails along this section were pulled up in 1979 as a result of a grant of abandonment by the Canadian Transport Commission. In 1977, the CPR abandoned part of the Osoyoos Subdivision, from Okanagan Falls to Osoyoos, due to the loss of fruit traffic to truck transport. What remained of the KVR ran three trains a week, serving the various sawmills, but by the mid-1980s a downturn in the forest industry saw all woodchip traffic lost to trucking. The final abandonment was in spring 1990, when track and bridges were removed. Some tunnels in the Coquihalla section were imploded by army engineers. This section saw the worst destruction, first from construction of the Trans Mountain pipeline through the pass, then from the Coquihalla Highway in the early 1980s, which obliterated the old rail bed.

After the abandonment of the Kettle Valley Railway, the Myra Canyon area was opened as a public recreational area until a disastrous fire in the summer of 2003 destroyed twelve of the wooden trestles and damaged two of the steel structures. The loss of the trestles and their significant historical and tourism values resulted in immediate public-private action to assess damage and develop options for rebuilding the trestles. Today, the Kettle Valley Steam Railway has been resurrected as a tourist attraction over a sixteen-kilometre section near the town of Summerland.

Andrew McCulloch enjoyed a long career that allowed him to preside over some of Canada's most exciting engineering projects of the time. Following his graduation from the Dominion Business College in Ontario, he worked as an axe man on the Great Northern Railway. By 1894, at the age of thirty, he was doing bridge work, then engineering for the CPR in the Crowsnest Pass before accepting the chief engineering position with KVR. After completing the line, he was appointed superintendent of operations for KVR, retiring in 1933 and working as a consultant until his death in 1945. McCulloch is buried in Penticton's Lakeview Cemetery, overlooking the Kettle Valley Railway to which he gave so much.

CHAPTER

5

Coring through the Cordillera

TUNNELLING WAS ESSENTIAL TO CREATING the most direct transcontinental rail route through the mountains, but it was not cheap in terms of human lives, time, or money. The steep, mountainous passage from BC to Alberta through the Selkirk and Rocky Mountain ranges proved to be by far the most expensive section of the national railway, fraught with hazards, extreme snowfalls, and seemingly impossible setbacks that would challenge CPR managers and engineers for decades to come. Under pressure to complete the rail link on time, the first engineers built long, winding routes on steep gradients that were difficult to travel on and maintain. Subsequent generations, with the benefit of new technologies, modified the route with safer gradients and a spectacular system of tiered tunnels. In due course they created a viable route through the majestic scenery of the Rockies that is recognized as a world-class example of high peaks railway engineering.

The engineers would begin with the western approach to Rogers Pass. Once the much-sought-after shortcut through the Selkirk Mountains, it would become the most costly pass on the line. Constructed during the 1880s at a cost of over $1 million, the single-track route wound through the narrow Illecillewaet Valley, twisting arduously up and over Rogers Pass before dropping into Beaver River Valley. This piece of track, marked by innumerable trestles, loops, and snowsheds, was expensive to maintain and was one of the biggest bottlenecks on the entire railway. With a summit of 1,311 metres, it was so steep that trains could barely make it to the top, and its tortuous twists and turns meant slow speeds. Because of the narrowness of the valley, it was not possible to twin the line to allow more than one train at a time.

In 1913, construction began on the first of a series of tunnels to widen the Rogers Pass route and improve its safety. The Connaught Tunnel (named for the Governor General at the time, Prince Arthur, Duke of Connaught) would pass directly under the Rogers Pass summit on Mount Macdonald. At eight kilometres, it was the longest railway tunnel in North America at the time. To construct it, a small tunnel was dug, into which crosscuts were made so that work could proceed at a number of sites simultaneously. The subcontractor guaranteed to drill 270 metres of tunnel per month, starting in April 1914, using a crew of three hundred men equipped with compressed air hand drills, jackleg drills ("jack" from the term used to describe an immigrant miner, and "leg" referring to the compressed-air cylinder used to change the angle of the drill as it vibrated against rock), and narrow-gauge locomotives. The tunnel was completed ahead of schedule and became operational in December 1916, after less than three years of construction.

The Connaught Tunnel eliminated the steepest part of the climb over the Selkirk Mountains and shortened the distance by more than six kilometres. Light at one end of the tunnel can be seen at the other. The cost was $5.5 million, with a further $3 million spent on measures to revise and shorten the surrounding track. The tunnel was later lined with reinforced concrete and equipped with a better ventilation system. Originally double tracked, it was realigned with a single central track in 1959 to accommodate taller freight cars and increased load capacities. Even so, it was still a bottleneck because westbound freight trains needed pusher engines to help them climb the 2.2 percent gradient (twenty-two metres of elevation for every kilometre travelled) preceding the tunnel. And air quality inside the tunnel was appalling, as multiple steam engines, straining to push their capacity loads through the eight kilometres of tunnel, filled the space with exhaust fumes that pushed out the fresh air. The introduction of diesel engines would help a bit, but not much.

Even with improvements and powerful diesels, the Rogers Pass section only allowed the passage of about fifteen westbound trains per day. Part of the problem was the steep eastward climb out of Beaver River Valley toward Kicking Horse Pass. Unable to twin the line to allow simultaneous eastbound and westbound traffic, engineers in the 1980s began investigating the potential for a second tunnel through Mount Macdonald. This new section of rail would be a combination of tunnels and fills cutting deep into the heart of the Selkirk peaks. The majority of the construction would take place within environmentally sensitive Glacier National Park, located at the summit of Rogers Pass. The route would need to accommodate a highway and a river through the narrow mountain valley and be built in such a way as to maintain the visual and natural integrity of the park.

And so the Rogers Pass Project was begun, the largest CPR undertaking since completion of the transcontinental railway in 1885. The $500-million project would cover 34 kilometres in total, including 17 kilometres of surface route, six bridges totalling 1.7 kilometres in length, and two tunnels. The centrepiece of the project would be the 14.6-kilometre Mount Macdonald Tunnel, cored through the Macdonald and Cheops Mountains. A second tunnel through Mount Shaughnessy would pass under the Trans-Canada Highway. Preparatory work began in 1982, with construction beginning in mid-1984. Crews blasted in from the west end and burrowed in from the east, using a huge mechanical rotary excavator called the "mole." On October 24, 1986, the two crews met in the middle.

The Macdonald Tunnel features the first use in North America of a concrete "Pact-Track" floor system, eliminating the need for wooden railway ties and crushed rock ballast, thus reducing maintenance costs. The tunnel interior is 5.1 metres wide and 7.8 metres high. It was surveyed using laser and satellite technology and built to accommodate any future electrified railway. The Macdonald Tunnel crosses the alignment of the Connaught Tunnel 110 metres below. A ventilation system with a ventilation shaft to the summit, four 1.68-megawatt fans, and an external building with gates, controls, and monitoring system, was installed to remove smoke and diesel pollutants from the tunnel. Instruments are in place to constantly monitor the exact position of trains and the ventilation conditions. The entire length of the main track is lined with a smooth reinforced-concrete surface that reduces wind resistance when a train passes through.

Meanwhile, up on the surface, three box culverts and five bridges divert the flow of cascading mountain streams away from the tunnel. Water dammed up against the base of a railway or highway will cause washouts. For this reason, culverts are used to drain away water, or, at least, to equalize the quantity of water on each side. There are three types of culvert—arch, box, and pipe. For this project, rail engineers chose to use a concrete rectangular-cross-section box culvert, which has a greater capacity than either of the other two.

The interiors of both the Mount Macdonald Tunnel and the 1.8-kilometre-long Mount Shaughnessy Tunnel (a.k.a. Rogers Pass Short Tunnel) are illuminated with high-pressure sodium lights. Because these lights are on continuously, grain spilled from passing trains has been found to sprout up to ten centimetres high. The west end of the Mount Shaughnessy Tunnel had to be reinforced with steel and concrete because of brittle, loose rock in the area. The walls along the remainder of the tunnel have a lining, or "skin," of sprayed concrete. Because of the mountain's dense, gravelly loam, field instruments were installed so engineers could monitor the ground and lining for any shifts in behaviour during and after construction.

A major challenge in this phase of the Rogers Pass reconstruction was that it had to be completed on slopes of up to forty degrees. Cutting into the cliff would create ugly scars that would compromise the scenery and undermine the existing rail line. The solution was to construct a viaduct that could support the rails along the cliff face without causing too much damage to the valley. The 1,229-metre-long viaduct near the top of Beaver River Valley has forty-five steel bridge spans, forty-four piers, and two abutments. The piers are anchored nine metres into bedrock. Heading east, the viaduct begins just west of Stoney Creek Bridge and ends a few metres from the east portal of the Mount Shaughnessy Tunnel.

The completion of the Rogers Pass Project in 1988 doubled the line's capacity. Westbound CPR trains could now go through the Mount Macdonald Tunnel while eastbound trains used the Connaught Tunnel. The grade on the eastern approach was reduced to only 0.95 percent, eliminating the need for pusher engines. Through innovative engineering, the CPR had eliminated a steep, costly, and deadly section of the Rogers Pass line and built what was then the longest railway tunnel in North America.

* * *

Kicking Horse Pass has always been a transportation headache. Located at an elevation of 1,635 metres, it spans the provincial border between Lake Louise in Alberta and Field, British Columbia. It is a national historic site of Canada and a major rail and highway corridor through the Rocky Mountains. The pass is the point at which the Canadian Pacific Railway and Trans-Canada Highway cross the Continental Divide (a.k.a. Great Divide), where rivers on one side flow west to the Pacific Ocean and rivers on the other side flow east to Hudson's Bay and the Atlantic Ocean. Today, the pass is a construction-scape of engineering artifacts: rail beds; rails, grades, and curves; snowsheds, tunnels, and runaway sidings; rock cuts; abandoned work camps; and equipment.

Mount Stephen Tunnel in Upper Kicking Horse Pass, *circa* 1886–88.
GLENBOW ARCHIVES NA-1753-39

The original line surveyed for Kicking Horse Pass in the 1880s extended from Wapta Lake to Ottertail Station across a number of avalanche paths. It would have required a 427-metre tunnel through the "nose" of Mount Stephen; however, uncertainty about the stability of the terrain, and the added time and cost needed to build such a line, necessitated an alternate route. With time and money in short supply, CPR civil engineers decided against a tunnel, opting instead to build over the top of Mount Stephen. Too late, they discovered that the summit drops off precipitously, leaving no room for lengthening the line or reducing the downhill grade through Kicking Horse Canyon.

Federal rail standards required a 2.2 percent maximum

rail gradient, but Van Horne had already informed the government it would take an extra year of drilling to get a roadbed if engineers had to adhere to the standard. Anxious to get the transcontinental line completed, the government gave permission to push on regardless. In spite of a late start in spring 1884 because of deep snow, the CPR navvies managed to get the job done, but at a whopping 4.4 percent gradient, when no other railway had ever exceeded 2.2 percent. They laid track in a steep descent from the top of the pass to Field, BC, dropping 115 metres for every kilometre. The 6.6-kilometre-long "Big Hill" section between Field and Hector, with a grade of 4.4 percent over eight kilometres and 3.5 to 4 percent over the remaining distance, was a "temporary solution" to carry the line down the Kicking Horse Canyon.

It was a temporary solution that lasted for twenty-five years and caused monumental problems and expense. The hill was too steep for descending westbound trains to maintain controlled braking or ascending eastbound trains to power up over the top. It operated like an out-of-control roller coaster ride. The route up from Lake Louise was a worrisome crawl where the trains were in constant danger of stalling and slipping backward into the valley. But this was just a rehearsal for the cardiovascular tune-up of roaring down the other side to Field, a stretch in which massive breakaway trains could fly right off the rails. On the route out of Field, it took four locomotives to get an average 650-tonne load of freight up the twelve-kilometre hill to Hector. Trains were limited to twelve to seventeen freight or eleven passenger cars, and it took a time-consuming hour to cover the twelve kilometres.

In a series of efforts to ameliorate the problem, switch-backs were added, extra pusher locomotives were coupled at the rear of uphill-bound trains, and brakes were vigorously tested before the downhill trip. The speed on descent was limited to ten kilometres per hour. Dining and sleeping cars had to be unhitched to lighten the load on ascent, forcing the CPR to build passenger rest stops at Mount Stephen House and Glacier House, similar to those in the Fraser Canyon. Freight trains were shortened, and still many disastrous crashes occurred. Not only was the Kicking Horse Pass route dangerous, it was inefficient and expensive, requiring more locomotives and extra crews to get the trains through. All of these factors added up to create a serious bottleneck on the transcontinental line.

Powerful steam locomotives with exotic names like 2-8-2 Mikado, 4-6-2 Pacific, 2-10-2 Santa Fe, and 2-10-0 Decapod were the workhorses that kept Canadian commerce moving through Kicking Horse Pass. The locomotives were categorized by their wheel arrangement through a system called the Whyte notation, named for Frederick Methvan Whyte, a Dutch mechanical engineer from the New York Central Railway. Numbers are assigned to the leading, driving, and trailing wheels of the locomotive. The first number refers to the number of leading wheels, the middle to the number of drivers, and the last to the number of trailing wheels (typically located under the firebox). For example, a 2-8-4 means that there are two leading wheels (one axle), eight driving wheels (four axles), and four trailing wheels (two axles). A zero means there are no trailing wheels.

When trains arrived at the pass, special "hill crews" would take over from the regular crew to shunt both passenger and freight cars down to Field or up to Lake Louise. Usually they worked in tandem teams or were positioned at either end of a short train as they manoeuvred along the difficult passage. Special locomotives with water brakes that were better equipped to absorb mechanical energy than either lever or vacuum systems were purchased and stationed at Field. The town of Field had originally been called the Third Siding until December 1884, when the CPR named it after C.W. Field, a Chicago businessman whom they hoped to flatter into investing in their railroad.

The first train to attempt the Big Hill in 1884 derailed, tragically killing three workers. Following the incident, three reverse-grade runaway sidings were created at 1.6-kilometre intervals to divert and slow speeding trains. Switches were set for the emergency exit sidings and were not reset to the main line until switchmen knew the oncoming train was under control, indicated by the engineer's blast of four short whistles. Still, train wrecks happened. In 1889, a fourteen-car coal train pulled by locomotive No. 314, one of the more powerful 2-8-0 Consolidation models used in the Kicking

Horse Valley, lost brake power and came thundering down the hill. The switchman at the second safety siding believed the train had whistled for the main line and let it through. Just before the train derailed, the crew jumped for their lives. A brakeman was killed, and the fireman died of his injuries later. Locomotive 314 was rebuilt and returned to service. In 1894, while pushing a freight train up the hill three kilometres east of Field, the boiler blew, killing the engineer, fireman, and conductor. The remains of No. 314 were salvaged and it was rebuilt once again and returned to service on the Big Hill. In 1907, it was renumbered to 1320, then in 1912 to 3120. It was scrapped in 1917 after thirty-one years in service. Its dome, ripped off in the 1894 explosion, was placed in the Lower Spiral Tunnels viewing area on the Trans-Canada Highway eight kilometres east of Field in Yoho National Park.

CHAPTER

6

The Schwitzer Solution

THE SPIRAL TUNNELS NEAR FIELD, BC, are an engineering feat unique in North America. They were the CPR's solution to halving the grade of the Big Hill descent by doubling the distance. This was achieved in 1909 through the construction of two tunnels through Mount Ogden and Cathedral Mountain, which reduced the gradient from 4.4 percent to 2.2 percent. Inspired by the Baischina Gorge tunnels in Switzerland, John Edward Schwitzer, an assistant chief engineer for CPR's western lines, created this masterpiece of engineering by designing a pair of looping tunnels in a figure-eight pattern. An eastbound train leaving Field climbs a moderate hill, passes through two short, straight tunnels on Mount Stephen, under the Trans-Canada Highway, across the Kicking Horse River, and into the Lower Spiral Tunnel through Mount Ogden. Once inside, it spirals upward and to the left for 891 metres, emerging 15 metres higher from where it entered. The train then crosses back over the Kicking Horse River, under the highway a second time, and into a 991-metre tunnel in Cathedral Mountain. There, it spirals to the right, emerging 17 metres higher, and continues to the top of Kicking Horse Pass. In all, the line crosses the valley three times and the Kicking Horse River four times on four different bridges.

The construction of the Spiral Tunnels took two years, from 1907 to 1909, and required one thousand workers, $1.5 million, and the excavation of 54,000 cubic metres of rock. All four tunnel entrances were started at the same time. Without the luxury of modern technology or computers, workers carved out the tunnels from both ends, finishing at the centre within five centimetres of their targeted point of completion. By the way, the story that Schwitzer realized a week before the tunnelling was complete that his calculations were off and the shafts would never meet is an urban legend. His numbers were correct. He did not shoot himself in a fit of despair. He went on to create other engineering marvels.

One of these was the Lethbridge Viaduct, also known as the High Level Bridge, designed by Schwitzer as part of a 1907 project to improve the section of rail along the Oldman River. At 1,624 metres long and 96 metres high, and supported on thirty-three steel towers, it is the largest

Route followed by CPR trains through the Spiral Tunnels in Kicking Horse Pass. From the CPR menu cover, *circa* 1920–29.

GLENBOW ARCHIVES NA-4594-1

railway trestle bridge in Canada and the largest of its type in the world. The design and scale of the viaduct were unprecedented in the early twentieth century. The spans between towers are twenty metres long, with thirty-metre intermediate spans, considered a phenomenal length at the time. The use of partial through-plate girder spans was also uncommon, and having part of the girder higher than the rail provided a partial wind buffer on the high structure. Along with a second bridge over the Oldman River west of Monarch, the new route, which opened in 1909, eliminated many curves in the old line and reduced the grade from 1.2 percent to only 0.4 percent, while reducing the track length by 8.5 kilometres.

With the opening of the Spiral Tunnels, the lofty lodgings that had been constructed for passengers to disembark at so their trains could make it up the Big Hill were repurposed as high-altitude accommodations for wealthy adventure travellers from Europe and the east. The CPR built two types of accommodation: urban hotels near major passenger stations and rural destination resorts in areas with unique scenery. This latter category included the smaller alpine-themed hotels, or "stationary dining cars," that had provided food services to passengers without the train having to haul heavy dining and kitchen cars over mountain peaks. In 1886, three of these were in operation: Mount Stephen House at Field, BC, in Yoho National Park, Glacier House in Rogers Pass, and Fraser Canyon House at North Bend (Boston Bar). As travellers began to explore some of these areas' natural wonders, such as the limestone Nakimu Caves (a Shuswap word meaning "grumbling spirits") in Cougar Brook Valley, the demand for overnight visits increased, and the rest stations were quickly developed. At Great Glacier (Illecillewaet Glacier) in Rogers Pass, the dining hall was supplemented by chalet rooms. These booked up so quickly that others were soon added. Meals were seventy-five cents (the same as in dining cars), and rooms one dollar a night. A sleeper car was parked on the siding until extra rooms could be built, along with climbers' cabins, tea houses, and hiking trails, which would soon gain the region status as the cradle of North American mountaineering.

In 1899, the CPR took further steps to promote tourism by advertising Canada's mountains as "50 Switzerlands in One" and importing two Swiss guides, Christian Haesler Sr., and Edward Feuz Sr., from Interlaken Switzerland ("sturdy picturesque fellows"), to teach safe climbing techniques at Glacier House. Back in 1883, with one eye to future profits and the other on the successful American partnership between Northern Pacific Railway and Yellowstone National Park created in 1872, Van Horne had proposed the designation of national parks along the Rocky Mountain line, an area he called "the climax of mountain scenery." The Canadian government complied, establishing Banff National Park in 1885, followed by Glacier and Yoho National Parks in 1886. Railway construction had other economic spinoffs. Rogers Pass was soon transformed from wilderness to the bustling Summit City, complete with hotels, saloons, barbershop, general store, school, and houses, plus rail-maintenance yards at Rogers Station. Mining claims were staked and timber rights registered. The mountains were in business.

The CPR hotel at Lake Louise (later called Chateau Lake Louise) gained notoriety in 1896 when Philip Stanley Abbot, a Boston lawyer and climber, had the misfortune to fall off Mount Lefroy while free climbing to the summit, thus achieving the dubious distinction of being North America's first mountaineering casualty. The climbing equipment of the time was basically hemp rope, hobnail boots, and an ice axe—no pitons or carabiners that a climber would use today.

Over time, the CPR's first two Swiss guides were supplemented by some thirty-five more, until 1954. The guides assisted guests in getting up, and off, the summits safely; later, they worked as ski instructors at the resorts. A stone refuge cabin for mountaineers, tucked in the saddle between Mount Lefroy and Mount Victoria, was constructed by Swiss guides in 1922. Both the hut and the pass were named in honour of the unfortunate Mr. Abbot. Materials were hauled by horses across the Lower Victoria Glacier and then carried on the guides' backs the rest of the way. Cement, lime, windows, timbers, tools, beds, bedding, and a stove were carried the same way from Lake Louise via the route known as the "Death Trap," so named for an incident involving the guide Edward Feuz Jr. While passing over the glacier, Feuz and others were swept down by an avalanche. All were located; Feuz was found with only his hand sticking out of the snow. After he was dug out, his first concern was that he had lost his pipe in the "darned [or something close] avalanche."

Built with local construction materials and a Swiss design, the high-roofed Abbot Pass hut in Glacier National Park blends with its natural environment. The hut is constructed from locally quarried, hand-cut stone and is an example of the rustic design tradition popular in the early 1900s. The second highest such structure in Canada, at an altitude of 2,925 metres (the highest is Neil Colgan hut, at 2,957 metres, in Kootenay National Park), the hut serves as a base for mountaineers attempting to ascend Mount Lefroy and Mount Victoria, both over 3,400 metres high. Abbot Pass Hut is a national historic site and one of twenty-four high-alpine bases operated by the Alpine Club of Canada.

While people were trying to climb mountains, railcars were trying to climb steep gradients. Even with the completion of the Spiral Tunnels, which eliminated the Big Hill, there were still the Field Hill and other sections to the east and west of Field to be tamed. On these sections, it was necessary to add extra locomotives for power and traction to help trains over the 2.2 percent gradients. Yes, it was the standard incline, but it was still tough going. This was mountain topography, not prairie grassland. The Ottertail revision of 1902, which kept the line at river level below Field, and the double-tracked Connaught Tunnel of 1916 were other improvements to the original line. Even so, bigger steam locomotives were needed, and six massive 0-6-6-0 articulated Mallet models with extra driving axles were purchased, the first in 1909, and five more in 1911. More powerful still were the fourteen 2-10-2 (Santa Fe type) locomotives built in 1919–20 and the twenty 2-10-4 Selkirk models, the most powerful steam locomotive in the British

Empire, purchased in 1929. Another ten locomotives were added in 1938 and a final six in 1949. The last steam train to pass through the Spiral Tunnels was a BC Rail excursion train pulled by Royal Hudson No. 2860 in April 1979. Diesel electric engines came into transcontinental use, and over the decades bigger and more powerful models replaced smaller ones, as was the case with their predecessors, the steam locomotives.

Today, trainspotters can see diesel engines pulling upwards of one hundred railcars through the Spiral Tunnels from a viewpoint on the Trans-Canada Highway in Yoho National Park between Field and the summit of Kicking Horse Pass. If the train is long enough, it is possible to see both ends at the same time. It will appear to spiral over itself as the engine leaves one portal while the rear car has yet to enter the other. This spot has been called the "bow" in Canada's transcontinental ribbon of rail and is a favourite with photographers. The viewpoint (closed October–April) also has exhibits showing how the tunnels work. The Spiral Tunnels were used on a regular basis for freight and travellers until 1990, when VIA Rail ceased regular passenger service through them, although tourist runs are still conducted by companies like the Rocky Mountaineer.

CHAPTER

7

Bridging the Waters

THE HIGH PEAKS OF THE Rocky and Selkirk mountain ranges were challenging for the CPR engineers, but so was the large number of raging rivers. Paying, housing, and feeding crews on massive construction projects through mountains and across river valleys almost bankrupted the company. To save money, in 1884 the CPR stopped building in masonry and steel and shifted to wooden structures, with bridge trestles assembled from trees chopped down close to the worksite. No other railway in the history of North America built as many high timber bridges as the CPR did for its initial push through the Rockies. Untreated wood did not last as long as steel, but the objective was to lay track and get the line open.

Some of the most spectacular bridges built by the CPR were the three timber structures spanning Stoney, Mountain, and Surprise Creeks in an area near the Columbia River where the line turns toward Beaver River Valley. The highest timber bridge ever built, and the second highest in North America at the time of its construction in 1885, was the original Stoney Creek truss bridge. At an elevation of ninety metres, it carried the CPR's upper line over a deep gully in Rogers Pass through what is now Glacier National Park.

The truss bridge, one of the oldest styles of bridges, is basically a structure of connected rigid timbers, or iron rods, forming triangular units. The bridge's simple design allowed stresses to be readily calculated by nineteenth-century engineers, and they were economical to build. Massachusetts millwright William Howe first patented his design for heavy-duty bridge spans in 1840. The Howe truss used mostly wood in its construction and was suitable for long spans. The Pratt truss used more iron, which was costly to manufacture and transport. The Howe design was adopted by the railway industry and became one of the most widely used trusses for railroad bridges, especially in western North America, where wood, although prone to fire and decay, was plentiful.

While the Howe truss includes vertical members and diagonals that slope upward toward the centre, the Pratt truss does the opposite, with vertical members and diagonals that slope downward. The Howe truss used wooden beams for the diagonal members, which are in compression, and iron (later steel) for the vertical members, which are in tension. The Pratt truss was the opposite, and since diagonal members are longer, the Howe truss did not require as much expensive iron. By using the Howe system, the CPR could supplement trusses made from unseasoned wood harvested on site with smaller quantities of iron. Iron bridge members could then be adjusted to accommodate the shrinkage or warping of the wood as it aged and dried. At Stoney Creek, the trusses measured fifty-two metres and forty-nine metres. Both spans shared a central pier sixty metres high.

Like many wood bridges that are seldom meant to be permanent, the Stoney Creek Bridge was replaced in 1893–94 by a steel-arch bridge with a 102-metre central span anchored in two rocky cliffs. Years later, the bridge was reinforced for heavier locomotives by adding extra truss arch ribs next to each of the two original trusses and replacing the deck spans with smaller girder spans and additional spandrel supports (connecting rods in the triangular area between the bridge arch and the rail track above). The arch alone uses 475 tonnes of steel out of a total weight of 700 tonnes. In 1929, the bridge was again reinforced with new deck girders, supports, and additional arches. It remains a favourite with scenic photographers to this day.

Nearby Mountain Creek Bridge, a timber behemoth at 366 metres long and 53 metres high, and Surprise Creek Bridge, at 48 metres high, were the second- and third-highest

The Mountain Creek Bridge near Beaver River Valley, BC, *circa* 1885.
GLENBOW ARCHIVES NA-782-13

timber bridges on the CPR main line. Steel trestles replaced wood at Surprise Creek in 1894 and at Mountain Creek in 1902. However, the reinforcements were not enough to prevent the collapse of the Surprise Creek Bridge in 1929 as a locomotive was crossing, killing both engineers in the cab. The stone-arch Cascade Creek Bridge on the original CPR line near Stoney Creek can now be viewed from the Rogers Pass east picnic area and forms part of the national historic site there. No other timber bridge would ever be built as high as the first Stoney Creek Bridge.

James Ross was the Scotsman in charge of construction for the CPR Mountain Division. His responsibility was to supervise the building of the most difficult section of the main line over the Rocky and Selkirk ranges to link up with Onderdonk's waiting rail. By spring 1885, Ross's crews were poised to move up Beaver River Valley in the east Selkirks and tackle Rogers Pass. Specifically, they had to span the open gorges through which Mountain, Surprise, Stoney, and Cascade Creeks ran and join them up as part of the main line. At Mountain Creek, they built a wooden trestle bridge stretching across the valley for 331 metres at 50 metres above the rushing water below. A few kilometres farther up the line at Stoney Creek, they constructed their masterpiece, a bridge that towered 64 metres on top of its substantial footings. But it was slow work. At one point, forest fires from lightning strikes not only kept them from working in large sections of forest, but consumed vast quantities of construction material. Finally, storms came through and rain quenched the flames, but then the downpours would not stop. It rained for days on end, and the already rapidly flowing mountain streams became swollen, their runoff gouging out bridge underpinnings as fast as they could be rebuilt. The men had to contend with oozing mud, washouts along the supply trails, and unstable, waterlogged embankments. These hardships did not seem as bad to Ross and his crews as an old danger new to navvies working in the mountains— overhanging snow on high ridges that came thundering down the slopes to wipe out everything in its path.

The Columbia Mountains, which include the Monashees and Selkirks, capture Pacific moisture coming across the BC

Interior Plateau. As a result, they receive some of the largest snowfalls in the country. The snow in Rogers Pass is legendary, with snowpacks that can become over thirty metres deep. Along isolated ridges and steep hillsides, these heavy masses can become unstable and thunder wildly down into valleys below. With the advent of railway construction, these areas were no longer isolated.

A snowslide, or avalanche, is a force of nature with the power to snap the trunks of huge trees into kindling or pick up boulders and men and hurl them downhill at speeds of up to three hundred kilometres an hour. People can be crushed under tonnes of snow packed as hard as concrete, or suffocate before they can be dug out. Local First Nations respected the power of avalanches and avoided the backcountry until the danger period had passed. But construction crews ignored the elements, at their peril, and continued creating noise and vibrations as they worked, watching, listening, and hoping the "white death" would not descend upon them. Back in February 1885, seven men had been buried in avalanches and rescued, but two had been killed. Ross wrote to Van Horne, "The men are frightened. I find the snowslides on the Selkirks are much more serious than I anticipated, and I think are quite beyond your ideas of their magnitude and danger to the line."

Ross reached the summit of Rogers Pass on August 17, 1885, but he then faced laying track on the westward descent to the Columbia River. The route through the

Illecillewaet Valley was troublesome. On the north side, they would have to contend with steep grades and avalanche debris. Continuing on that trajectory would expose the tracks to several more dangerous avalanche slopes. But the south side presented such a short, steep gradient that it was an invitation to train wrecks and death. They had already been through a similar situation in Kicking Horse Pass and did not wish a repeat. Ross solved his engineering problem by constructing an intricate series of three rail loops in the valleys of Glacier Creek, Loop Creek, and the Illecillewaet River. This brought the gradient down to the maximum allowable of 2.2 percent. By adding sixteen kilometres of additional track, Ross was able to reduce it further to eighteen metres per kilometre, or 1.8 percent. From here, he proceeded to cross the Columbia River at a location that would later become the site of Revelstoke. The route continued west to Eagle Pass in the Gold Range of the Monashee Mountains, where it would meet up with the end of steel coming from the Pacific.

* * *

The Cisco Bridges are a pair of railroad bridges at Siska (historically called Cisco), on the Fraser River south of Lytton, BC, where the CPR and CNR tracks run on opposite sides of the Fraser River. At this point, the trains switch sides. The CPR arrived first, in 1884, and chose the easier route. When the CNR arrived later, it was not possible to squeeze two lines onto the same side of the narrow canyon, so a second, more difficult route, had to be built along the other side of the canyon. The Cisco Bridges are located at the point where the two sections pass one another. The area is popular with trainspotters and photographers because the proximity of the two bridges allows both to be in the same frame, with the occasional bonus of a train on each bridge simultaneously. The CPR's steel and stone bridge (reinforced in 1908–09 to handle 9,000-tonne trains using it daily) is a three-span cantilever truss link, 161 metres long and 43 metres above the low-water level. It lies adjacent to the 181-metre-long Cisco tunnel, which enters the Cisco Bluff at the southern (downstream) crossing. The CNR bridge is a 247-metre-long, 90-metre-high truss arch bridge on the northern side. The Trans-Canada Highway runs parallel to the two bridges down the east bank of the Fraser River.

Canada has a number of bridges with heritage value, and while the first impressive structures were built for the transcontinental railroad, the engineers of the Trans-Canada Highway project also needed to bridge some impressive geography in the mid-twentieth century. Ainslie Creek, which enters the Fraser River Canyon north of Boston Bar, cut a deep ravine into the land. The highest arch bridge and second-highest bridge overall on the 1,039- kilometre Trans-Canada Highway, the Ainslie Creek Bridge, also known as Nine Mile Canyon, is a steel-truss arch 91 metres high with a main span of 146 metres. Constructed in 1958, the bridge runs parallel to the CN rail line but more than 30 metres above it. It was part of an overall improvement to the highway, which once crossed Ainslie Creek on a much lower timber bridge.

Highway and railway bridges often appear in proximity to each other, at points where both road and rail traffic must cross the same river. In 1961, British Columbia's premier, W.A.C. Bennett, opened the new 310-metre-long Columbia River Suspension Bridge on the Trans-Canada Highway at Revelstoke. Just south of this is the Canadian Pacific Railway Bridge, also over the Columbia River, and south of that is the 329-metre iron-truss Big Eddy Bridge, built in 1924. The Big Eddy Bridge replaced the original wooden train bridge built in 1910 and is named after a bend in the river by that name.

In 1964, the original four-lane Port Mann Bridge, which crosses the Fraser River near Surrey, BC, opened. At the time of construction, it was the most expensive section of highway in Canada. The community of Port Mann was originally known as Bon Accord, a steamboat landing on the Fraser River on the way up to Yale. Later, it became the northern terminus of the New Westminster and Southern Railway from the US. The name was changed to Port Mann to honour Sir Donald Mann, a builder, along with Sir William Mackenzie, of the Canadian Northern Railway.

Metro Vancouver's new Port Mann Bridge, which opened in December 2012, is the widest bridge in Canada and, at 470 metres, the second-longest cable-supported river crossing in North America. The final price tag for the project, including decommissioning the original bridge, maintenance, and debt repayment, was $3.3 billion, and it is one of the province's largest infrastructure projects ever, with road approaches covering thirty-seven kilometres from Langley to Vancouver.

High mountains and rushing waters are not just a challenge to bridge building. They are an opportunity for generating power. In addition to spanning rivers, engineers built dams to generate power and provide flood control. The Mica Dam on the Columbia River is one of the largest earth-fill dams in the world, rising to a height of 244 metres above bedrock. Completed in 1973, it is located near the former settlement of Mica, now flooded under the dam's reservoir, Kinbasket Lake (formerly McNaughton Lake). In addition to power generation, the Mica Dam was built to provide 8.6 cubic kilometres of water storage under terms set by the Columbia River Treaty, plus another 6.2 cubic kilometres of "non-treaty storage."

The nearby Revelstoke Dam rises 175 metres over the Columbia River. The dam, which began operation in 1984, caused the formation of the reservoir known as Lake Revelstoke. The powerhouse, with five generating units, has a capacity of 2,480 megawatts. The Revelstoke Dam Visitor Centre offers tours of the dam and exhibits on the history and science of hydroelectric operations.

Bridging the Waters

Three high bridges were built on the Mica Dam access road along Lake Revelstoke. Carnes Creek Bridge, at ninety-one metres high, crosses an inlet that was once a crevasse-like gorge before the waters were backed up by Revelstoke Dam. Constructed in 1982, the bridge is a four-span steel-girder overpass with a cantilevered central beam. Pier number two of the bridge rises seventy-seven metres above the south bank of the gorge. Nearby Mars and La Forme Creek Bridges are similarly high, rising fifty-eight metres above the old creek levels.

Both the Revelstoke and Mica dams inundated the Big Bend Highway, the original route of the Trans-Canada Highway until the Rogers Pass section was completed in 1962. Thanks to a sophisticated network of snowsheds and avalanche-control programs, the drive through Rogers Pass from Golden to Revelstoke is now relatively safe from the "white death" that claimed the lives of so many during the thirty years the CPR used the pass.

For rail, bridge, and highway engineers, the mountains and passes that the First Nations had treated with such respect became barriers to be conquered by modern transportation technology. The dangers have been reduced, but not eliminated. The views are spectacular and much enhanced by the experience of travelling on a precarious route with steep drop-offs on one side and the possibility of cascading rocks or snow from above. It is exciting and, for the most part, safe.

CHAPTER

8

Danger Above and Below

AN AVALANCHE IS A WONDER to behold—but not close up, if you intend to see a second one. Indicators for assessing the stability of a snowpack include temperature, humidity, wind speed and direction, underlying terrain, depth of freshly fallen snow, and even the shape of snow crystals. To the trained mountaineer, they are obvious, but to rookie rail crews and wilderness tourists, they are often too subtle to be noticed until it's too late.

Avalanches and rock slides block rail lines. Flash floods and erosion undermine rail lines. Aggressive vegetation growth impedes train movement along rail lines. It was vitally important to keep the single thin line of rail through the mountains open year-round, even with up to twelve metres of snowfall and avalanches tearing away newly laid track. The CPR had to build diversion structures to protect the country's newest communication link, and it had to build a lot of them. Snowsheds and rock sheds are necessary, especially in the Selkirks, where warm, moist Pacific air collides with the frigid peaks, resulting in a high volume of overhanging snowdrifts that become unstable and can come roaring down, wiping trains off tracks, killing passengers, and destroying freight. In summer, the accumulation of loose debris from winter avalanches combined with spring runoff can result in rock slides that are equally catastrophic. The solution was to construct massive timber snowsheds of Douglas fir—literally, wooden tunnels with sloping roofs— to shield the vulnerable rail line.

In the CPR's ongoing snow war, the construction of a costly system of thirty-one snowsheds was begun in 1886 over the most exposed section of Rogers Pass, a segment extending 6.5 kilometres along Connaught Creek and the Illecillewaet River. But this was only a small portion of the route, and crews were frequently dispatched to dig out buried lines between snowsheds.

Over 250 men died in avalanches in Rogers Pass between 1885 and 1911. The worst event occurred just before midnight on March 4, 1910. A crew of fifty-eight men and a rotary snowplow operator were moving snow from a previous avalanche on Cheops Mountain just south of Shed 17. The plow had cut a path through the snow and the men were working in the cut, shovelling snow and clearing out trees swept along by the avalanche. Suddenly, a second avalanche accelerated down the aptly named Avalanche Mountain on the other side of the valley. The men had been working hard through the night and hadn't had time to focus on the elements. The westbound CPR train No. 97 had just entered the Rockies, bound for Vancouver, and this was its only route. The unanticipated avalanche entombed all of the men, and some four hundred metres of track were buried. The eighty-two-tonne locomotive was tossed fifteen metres and landed upside down. The wooden freight cars behind the locomotive were reduced to a pile of splinters.

When news of the accident reached Revelstoke, a rescue train with 200 workers and all available doctors and nurses was sent to the scene. Another train with a rescue team of 125 left from Calgary. When they arrived, all was quiet. There were no injured. There were two more avalanches in the next two days. One, 3.2 kilometres from the disaster, buried the track under eighteen metres of snow. But within days, 800 workers were at the accident site, digging out the track and uncovering bodies. Many of the dead were recovered in an upright position reminiscent of the residents of Pompeii in the first century AD, frozen in time in layers of volcanic ash from the cataclysmic eruption of Mount Vesuvius. Only one man survived the avalanche. Billy Lachance, a locomotive fireman, had been blown out of the main debris field by the tornado-force winds that accompanied the onrush, which, as the Toronto *Globe* newspaper wrote on March 7, "whisked him a hundred feet through the air into the bush," from where he emerged banged up but alive. Among the dead were thirty-two Japanese immigrants from the Tokyo area who had been contracted to CPR by the Canada Nippon Supply Company in Vancouver. Howson's Funeral Parlour in Revelstoke received their bodies from the avalanche site and forwarded the remains to Vancouver, where most were buried in Mountain View Cemetery. The victims' families back in Japan received compensation ranging from $130 to $355. The CPR paid $47.50 per person to cover funeral costs and burial.

To keep more tragedies from happening, two types of barriers were constructed to divert dangerous snow and rock slides from above. One type, the snowshed, consisted of wooden galleries with roofs that followed the slope of the mountain. With the downward-angled shed roof in place to extend the slope of the mountains, avalanches could pass over the tracks without dumping their heavy load onto any unfortunate vehicle or person in their way. Snowsheds were expensive to build, but they were cheaper than tunnels and saved many lives. The second type of snow barrier consisted of high stone walls that prevented the rail line and snowshed from taking a direct hit from slides. Like the original railway trestles, each of these structures, some of which can still be seen in Rogers Pass, required massive amounts of timber for the beams and crossbeams. And, as with the trestles, wood would later be replaced by steel and concrete.

Effective as they were, snow structures tended to spoil the view, and tourists were becoming as important a railway payload as freight. The white hell in winter became scenic vistas in summer. In Glacier Park, so named because of its four hundred glaciers covering 10 percent of its area, the CPR built a second track outside the snowsheds so passengers could enjoy the view during the summer months while being protected during the winter months. Inside the park, which encompasses the craggy Columbia Mountains west of the Rockies, there can be fifteen to twenty metres of snow in winter, making it Canada's leading avalanche area, with snowslides reaching speeds up of to 325 kilometres per hour.

Another form of avalanche barrier is the snow bridge. These are rectangular panels fixed into rock by tension anchors on the upslope side and compression anchors on the downslope side of mountains. There are also snow fences, temporary barriers composed of thin, upright slats wired together to prevent snow from drifting onto roadways. Snow fences are vertical and accumulate snow on their downwind sides, while snow bridges are slanted, or horizontal, and hold snow on their top sides. Both are simple but practical static devices to protect both railways and highways from snowslides. Controls such as earthen mounds to stop or turn avalanches away, and catch basins, installed just above the right-of-way, were also employed, along with dikes, culverts, and dams, to recontour the landscape and collect snow and debris. In some areas, plants were encouraged to grow on the snow structures, providing more stability to better resist avalanches and rock slides. Then there were the mobile snow-moving devices created to push or throw snow out of the way. Rotary snowplows, with large circular rotating blades, bite through snow on the track. The few remaining rotary snowplows in North America are either in museums or used in areas with limited road access and high snowfalls, such as the Donner Pass in California and Japan's mountain passes. The early railways also used wedge snowplows with foldout wings (flanges), attached to the front of a locomotive. These could push through five-metre drifts and fling snow away in any chosen direction from the line. But they were slow and required the operators to continually make adjustments to the blade height in the midst of blowback. They also had to lift and lower the wings to avoid smashing obstacles near the tracks, such as rock cuts, bridge supports, and signposts.

The rotary plow was invented by Toronto dentist J.W. Elliot in 1869. Doesn't that just make you want to keep your next dental appointment? However, he never built a working model or prototype. The first rotary snowplow to be manufactured was designed by another Ontarian, named Orange Jull, who expanded on Elliot's design, building working models he tested with sand. During the winter of 1883–84, Jull contracted with Leslie Brothers of Toronto to build a full-size prototype that proved successful. Jull later sold his design rights to the Leslie Brothers, who formed the Rotary Steam Shovel Manufacturing Company in Paterson, New Jersey. The rotary snowplow uses a sloped steel casing to scoop snow from the tracks into a revolving fan located inside a wheel. The wheel is driven by a rotary engine on a shaft. Blades on the rim of the wheel catch the snow, which is propelled out through an opening at the top of the wheel. In 2001, the rotary snowplow was inducted into the North American Railway Hall of Fame in St. Thomas, Ontario, in the Technical Innovations category.

Huge wedge plows, rotary plows, snowsheds, and armies of shovellers still could not safely keep the rail line through Rogers Pass open in winter. Fighting the environment's steep grades and stormy weather year after year resulted in rising death tolls, schedule delays, and financial costs even higher than the surrounding peaks. Facing economic reality, the CPR was forced to take a different approach. The solution would be found in tunnel construction as a way of bypassing the formidable Rogers Pass summit. The tunnel under Mount Macdonald and other related improvements would be an expensive but more sustainable long-term solution to the costly battles year after year with Mother Nature. When the tunnel opened in 1916, the era of the original Rogers Pass rail summit, one of the world's most treacherous rail lines, had come to an end.

CHAPTER

9

The Transcontinental Footprint

BY 1883, THE RAILWAY LINE was coming together from both the east and the west, but the CPR was running out of money—again. So on January 31, 1884, the federal government passed the Railway Relief Bill, providing a further $22.5 million in loans to allow the work to continue. Overall, the CPR had been generously endowed by the federal government with cash, land grants, tax concessions, rights-of-way, and non-compete clauses, but it never seemed to be enough. The new technology was expensive, and the physical hurdles enormous.

Canada's western telegraph line was constructed in tandem with its rail line. Previously, telegraph messages (*tele* means "far" and *graph* means "write" in Greek) had to be sent via the US. Messages were written out by hand on blank forms and handed in for the operator to send. Telegraphy required the method for encoding and decoding a message to be known by both sender and receiver. In 1837, the American portrait painter-turned-inventor Samuel Morse developed and patented a standardized sequence of short and long signals called "dots" and "dashes" representing letters, numbers, and punctuation. The code's binary structure was simple to transmit, and the signal could cover great distances. Even if the cable was long and of poor quality, the message could be deciphered.

The telegraph was an enormous technological leap forward in speeding up business and personal communications. It was the social media of its day. In 1882, the CPR began selling its own telegraph services to offset the cost of constructing and maintaining its pole line. This sparked a revolution in connectivity. Thousands of kilometres of wire strung next to the tracks established crucial communication links between CPR managers as well as among communities throughout the new country. By following the national rail line, there was no need to negotiate transmission rights with many different landowners. The cost of telegraph construction was minor compared to rail construction, but still, lines had to be surveyed, holes dug, poles erected, cross arms and insulators attached, and wire tension adjusted. Once installed, the lines needed constant maintenance to ensure reliable operation.

The Transcontinental Footprint

In 1883, 133,000 immigrants arrived in Canada, and two-thirds of them continued west. Transporting them on a railway that was not yet complete was a problem for the CPR but a bonus for the new towns that were springing up along the rail line. For Aboriginal inhabitants of the prairie regions, the effects were devastating. The Blackfoot and Cree were shunted from their traditional lands and pressured to settle down and become farmers. The large herds of buffalo they relied on for subsistence were decimated through over-hunting by the settlers. Tensions came to a head when a group of Metis (people of mixed Aboriginal and European heritage) led by Louis Riel grew tired of having their grievances ignored by Ottawa and, in March 1885, declared their own provisional government in the District of Saskatchewan (Assiniboia). The uprising led to armed actions at Duck Lake and Frog Lake in which settlers and members of the local North West Mounted Police were killed. In the face of public anger over the insurrection, the federal cabinet of John A. Macdonald quickly changed its position against further funding of the railway and gave the go-ahead for Van Horne to finish construction and transport military troops to fight the Northwest Rebellion. But there were gaps in his railway. A total of 138 kilometres of track was missing in four different sections north of Lake Superior, and soldiers were on foot again when they reached the Metis strongholds at Qu'Appelle and Swift Current.

On March 30, 1885, the first troop train left Toronto.

At Dog Lake in northwestern Ontario, the first gap in the rail line, soldiers were piled into horse-drawn sleighs, which often overturned. Many suffered frostbite. At Birch Lake, there were no enclosed cars, so cold and wind chilled them to the bone. At Port Munro, the men marched over the ice of Lake Superior. One soldier wrote home, "We dared not stop an instant as we were in great danger of being frozen . . . One man of our company went mad and one of the regulars went blind from snow glare." The troops were on foot again for a sixteen-kilometre march over the melting ice of Nepigon Bay (now spelled Nipigon). The exhausted men stumbled forward, dragging those who could not get up. By the time they boarded the train for the last stretch, many could not swallow the hot tea they were served. Even with all their hardships, eight thousand troops got through in nine days. By comparison, it took troops three months to travel the same distance to put down the Red River Rebellion in 1869–70. Canada's forces defeated Riel at the Battle of Batoche on May 12, 1885, and a triumphant government approved further railway funding.

Every day during the summer and early autumn of 1885, the distance between the eastern and western rail lines grew shorter. The finish line would be at Eagle Pass, a gap in the Gold Range of the Monashee Mountains in British Columbia. It was Walter Moberly who, while exploring in 1865, gave the gap its name when he saw a convocation (group) of eagles flying through a break in the peaks. It is the point where Andrew Onderdonk, coming from the west, ran out of materials and ended his section of the trans-Canada line.

The town of Revelstoke, fifteen kilometres to the east of Eagle Pass, lies at the confluence of the Illecillewaet and Columbia Rivers. It was originally named Farwell after a local surveyor and landowner during the mining boom. In the 1880s, as the CPR first built through the area, they called it Second Crossing to differentiate it from the first crossing of the Columbia River at Donald, a divisional point west of Golden, BC. The town got its current name when CPR directors showed their gratitude to Edward Charles Baring, 1st Baron Revelstoke (Lord Revelstoke), head of Baring Brothers & Co. The British merchant bank had saved the CPR from bankruptcy in 1885 by buying up its unsold bonds, thus enabling the company to finance the railway to completion. Revelstoke's Baring Brothers bank, founded in 1762, collapsed in 1995 when a single employee lost £827 million ($1.3 billion) in speculative investments. On a non-monetary note, Lord Revelstoke was the great-great-grandfather of Diana, Princess of Wales.

Plans were underway for a joining-of-the-rails ceremony at Craigellachie, a spot in Eagle Pass named for a village of the same name on the River Spey in Moray, Scotland. Craigellachie was the ancestral home of Sir George Stephen, first president of the CPR. Sixteen years earlier, at the completion of the American transcontinental

Donald Smith drives home the "last spike" on November 7, 1885. Behind him to the left are Sandford Fleming (white beard) and W.C. Van Horne (black beard). Young Edward Mallandaine peers out from behind Smith's shoulder. CANADIAN PACIFIC ARCHIVES NS1960

railway in May 1869, the occasion was marked by the driving of a gold spike at Promontory Summit, Utah, and the transmission around the country of a one-word telegram— "Done." In Canada, Governor General Petty-Fitzmaurice, 5th Marquess of Lansdowne, was to bring a silver spike for the CPR ceremony. But, though he had travelled extensively through the Rockies by horseback and boat, this time inclement weather held him back. The final spike ended up being a conventional iron one. When it was suggested to Van Horne that he use a gold one, he replied, "The last spike will be just as good an iron one as there is between Montreal and Vancouver and anyone who wants to see it driven will have to pay full fare." Edward Mallandaine, a teenager from Victoria, hitched a ride on a CPR flatcar from Port Moody so he would arrive in plenty of time to see the tracks come together. While in Eagle Pass he saw "day by day the thousands of feet of earth removed and the swarms of men slaving away like ants for the good of the giant enterprise." Mallandaine was determined to get a good position where he could see the last spike driven to mark the end of the "giant enterprise." So, early in the morning of November 7, 1885, as the rails were almost touching, he inched forward through the group of burly men. Major A.B. Rogers cut the final rail at nine o'clock, and while one rail was spiked into place, the other was left loose with a spike inserted for the coming ceremony.

Under cloudy skies, Major Rogers held a tie bar under the final rail while Donald Alexander Smith (later Lord Strathcona), eldest of the four CPR directors present, picked up a spike maul and swung. Any one of his navvy spikers could have done better. It was a glancing blow that bent the spike. It had to be replaced. Smith picked up the hammer again. This time he struck it squarely. The official photograph, with Mallandaine peering over Smith's shoulder, was taken by Winnipeg photographer Alexander J. Ross. General Manager Van Horne and Sandford Fleming were among the small group of onlookers. Van Horne sent a telegram from a telegraph station conveniently located at Craigellachie to Prime Minister Macdonald in Ottawa that said, "Thanks to your far seeing policy and unwavering support the Canadian Pacific Railway is completed. The last rail was laid this (Saturday) morning at 9.22." Urged to make a speech, Van Horne kept it shorter than his telegram. "All I can say is that the work has been done well in every way." CPR dignitaries then boarded a train, which had travelled all the way from Montreal, and arrived the next day in Port Moody. There was no official party. British Columbia and the rest of Canada were joined. The promise had been kept.

In 1897 Edward Mallandaine staked a 477-square-kilometre land claim overlooking Kootenay Lake, where he helped establish the town of Creston and lived until his death in 1949. Lord Lansdowne's unused silver spike was presented to Van Horne. It remained in the hands of the Van Horne family until 2012, when they donated it, along with other artifacts, to the Canadian Museum of History in Ottawa.

Today in Craigellachie, a stone monument and little railway station mark the site of the "last spike." In 1938, a rock cairn was unveiled at Port Moody to commemorate the completion of the CPR to the Pacific. In fall 1885, however, the arrival of the dignitaries at Port Moody was not to be the end of the story. Upon landing, Van Horne surveyed the area around Port Moody and made the executive decision to move the CPR terminus to the Gastown area of Vancouver, a site he saw as better suited for servicing the company's steamships. Land was secretly acquired from the provincial government and local landowners to prevent speculators from scooping it up to resell at inflated prices. Rail crews extended the line a further eighteen kilometres west to the city. Engine No. 374 pulled the first passenger train into Vancouver on May 23, 1887.

The longest railway ever constructed at the time was supposed to take ten years but was completed in six. In all, it took 30,000 workers to complete the 3,200 kilometres of track across Canada. On July 4, 1886, the first through passenger train with 150 on board arrived in Port Moody after a journey of five days and nineteen hours from Montreal. It consisted of two first-class coaches, two sleeping cars, one second-class coach, two immigrant sleepers, a dining car, two baggage cars, and a mail car. Canada's national railway worked.

10

High-Level Highway

PUBLIC DEMAND FOR A NATIONAL roadway began as early as 1910, but it would be the middle of the twentieth century before construction got underway. In 1949, the federal Trans-Canada Highway Act fronted $150 million in start-up funds, half the initial estimated cost of construction. Cost-sharing plans with the provinces, revised twice, soon increased the federal portion to $825 million. Construction standards established for the highway called for low gradients and curvature; pavement widths of 6.7 metres and 7.3 metres; ample shoulder width, bridge clearances, and sight distances; elimination of railway grade crossings wherever possible; and a maximum load-bearing capacity of 8.2 tonnes per axle. Each province would be responsible for work within its own borders, and everything was to be wrapped up by December 1956.

As with the national railroad in the previous century, however, getting the job done was more complicated and more expensive than initially estimated. A range of engineering challenges delayed the highway's completion by six years. When it did officially open, in 1962, more than three thousand kilometres of the road were still unpaved gravel. Some sections were more problematic than others. One of these was the route through Rogers Pass between Golden and Revelstoke, an area that had claimed the lives of hundreds of CPR workers in the years before the rail tunnels were built through Mount Macdonald. Fortified with confidence and more mechanical technology than the original builders of the CPR could ever dream about, highway engineers tackled the mountainous terrain that had so challenged railway engineers. Initially, the highway followed the Columbia River around Big Bend, in order to avoid crossing Rogers Pass. With the opening of the Mica and Revelstoke Dams in 1964, this section of the valley was flooded, and so a new route had to be designed and built.

Once again, avalanches were the foe. The area's massive annual snowfalls required the construction of all manner of snowsheds, berms, and reinforced soil barriers for keeping the highway safe. Advance-warning systems were developed in tandem with concrete-and-steel open-galleried snowsheds. These were designed to deflect snow over the highway, not stop it, while protecting motorists as they toured and explored the mountains.

Farther east, the original twenty-six-kilometre section of highway through Kicking Horse Pass opened in 1962 as a twisting two-lane road, chopped out of sheer rock walls on one with hair-raising drop-offs to the river and rail line on the other side, leading to two narrow bridges over the Kicking Horse River. In 2007, these were replaced and realigned as part of the multi-phase Kicking Horse Canyon Project. The two major river crossings, Yoho Bridge and Park Bridge, now provide much safer and faster transit through the Rockies for both tourist and commercial traffic. The Kicking Horse improvements, begun in 2000, also included grade reduction, wildlife fencing/crossings, cycle paths, improvements to intersection design, a four-kilometre retaining wall east of Golden, and straightening and widening of the Golden Hill section from two lanes to four lanes. Total investment in the Kicking Horse Project came to over $958 million, for a key transportation corridor that carries ten thousand vehicles per day in summer. The Trans-Canada Highway reaches its greatest height in Kicking Horse Pass at an elevation of 1,643 metres.

In 1962 the Trans-Canada Highway was officially opened, twice. Ceremonies took place on the final stretch through Rogers Pass in Glacier National Park between Revelstoke and Golden. A provincial celebration was held on July 3, 1962, followed by a second federal-government commemoration ceremony on September 3. In a move reminiscent of Donald Smith driving the final spike on the Canadian Pacific Railway seventy-seven years earlier, Prime Minister John Diefenbaker tamped down a ceremonial patch of asphalt. While Smith had worn a black top hat to perform his official duties, Mr. Diefenbaker appeared in a business suit, polished shoes, and a new plastic hard hat balanced conspicuously on top of his head. He stated, "This highway, may it serve to bring Canadians closer together, may it bring to all Canadians a renewed determination to individually do their part to make this nation greater and greater still." This time, representatives from all ten provinces, as well as drivers anxious to travel the latest link, looked on as television cameras broadcast the event below the soaring peaks of Mount Macdonald and Mount Tupper, named for two Fathers of Confederation. A transport driver, A.D. Booth of Salmon Arm, BC, would be the first to bring 264 crates of fresh strawberries to Calgary produce buyers over the "spectacular new road." Previously, the shipment would have taken three days by rail.

A memorial arch in Glacier National Park at the Rogers Pass National Historic Site now commemorates the accomplishment of building a national roadway through dangerous mountain terrain under constant threat of the same "white death" avalanches, rock slides, raging rivers, and sheer cliffs that terrorized the builders of the national railway. The opening of the 7,821-kilometre Trans-Canada Highway meant people could now drive their own cars, instead of riding in railcars, from sea to sea. Using ferry services on both coasts, families and truckers could travel between St. John's, Newfoundland, and

Victoria, BC, along a single, unified highway system. Although there is no official starting point, and Canada converted to metric measurement in 1977, Victoria has placed a "Mile 0" monument to mark the start of the Trans-Canada Highway at the foot of Douglas Street and Dallas Road in Beacon Hill Park, while the city of St. John's has adopted the "Mile One" designation for its stadium and convention centre.

Today, a joint Parks Canada/National Defence mobile avalanche-control program, complete with snow-hazard forecasters and Canadian Forces gunners operating 105 mm. Howitzer artillery, keeps both road and rail passages through Rogers Pass open in winter. Designed to maintain public safety and minimize traffic delays, the program relies primarily on avalanche warnings, temporary road closures, and stabilization of avalanche slopes. Explosive charges are used to trigger small avalanches before enough snow can build up to cause a big avalanche. And the highway has something else the original railroad did not have: remote sensors above the pass that continually transmit weather conditions to a central forecast headquarters where staff can choose to close the highway and attack unstable slide areas in trigger zones high up in the avalanche path with a barrage of artillery fire. The shock waves from exploding shells set off avalanches under the right conditions. With the highway closed, they cascade harmlessly down into the valley.

In addition to active artillery control, seven permanent concrete avalanche sheds protect motorists travelling on the

Prime Minister John Diefenbaker at the opening of the Trans-Canada Highway, September 3, 1962. LIBRARY AND ARCHIVES CANADA E006580621

highway passing through Rogers Pass. The tunnels that allowed the railway to avoid the most active avalanche areas in the same pass have the added advantage of reducing environmental impacts on the summit. When roads are closed, motorists can wait in areas sheltered from avalanches. As traffic increases, additional passing lanes and possible lane twinning are anticipated. For tourists seeking a civilized wilderness adventure, it is now just a car ride away.

CHAPTER

11

Castles, Crags, and Caves

ARCHITECTURE CAN EITHER BE IMPOSED on a landscape or harmonious with it. Rocky Mountain developments have demonstrated a combination of both. Settlers arriving by horseback, ox cart, or rail had to build their own accommodations with materials at hand when they arrived, preferably before winter set in. Monied high-peaks tourists who arrived in the Rockies by rail were coddled in three architectural marvels: the (Fairmont) Banff Springs Hotel, Chateau Lake Louise, and Jasper Park Lodge. Rail passengers could enjoy lofty resort lodgings and outdoor adventure while contributing to the coffers of the CPR. These grand hotels were part of the nation-wide chain of railway hotels built by both the Canadian Pacific Railway and its less successful competitor, the Grand Trunk Railway. Most were located in city centres, but the Rocky Mountain hostelries used their unique locations to prime advantage.

Van Horne hired New York architect Bruce Price for his hotel project at Banff, originally called Siding 29. Price's Banff Springs Hotel, with its towers and turrets in a blend of French Château and Scottish Baronial style, quickly became the must-have architectural form for grand hotels and government buildings in Canada until the Second World War. Construction of the hotel, the tallest structure in the Rockies, began in spring 1887. Materials were hauled by wagon from the railway station in Banff. To shield the workers from snow and wind, an imposing enclosed scaffold was erected around the worksite. When Van Horne visited the site during construction, he noticed that the hotel was situated the wrong way—looking away from the majestic Bow River valley—so he quickly designed a viewing pavilion to be added for guests.

After just over a year of construction, at a cost of $250,000, the hotel opened in June 1888. Room rates started at $3.50 a day. In the first summer season, 1,503 guests visited, of whom 54 percent were Canadian, 26 percent American, 19 percent British, and 24 percent "other" nationalities. By 1911 there were 22,000 guests visiting per year. But it was not to last. The original structure, built from wood just like the early railway trestles, burned to the ground. Van Horne hired another American architect, Walter S. Painter, and two years later the rebuilding of the hotel by Italian stonecutters and Scottish masons was completed. The new building was made from locally quarried Rundle stone, a brittle sedimentary limestone obtained from the base of Mount Rundle about two kilometres away. The structure earned the name "Castle in the Wilderness," alternatively referred to as "Castle in the Rockies." Today, the grey-brown and black stone used for building and landscaping is excavated near Canmore, Alberta.

The first non-Aboriginal person to see Lake Louise (altitude 1,731 metres) was CPR horse wrangler/packer Tom Wilson, who, with Stoney guides, camped near its eastern shore in 1882. During the night he heard the roar of an avalanche. Using his limited Stoney vocabulary, Wilson managed to discern that the noise was coming from "snow mountains above the lake of little fishes." The next day he rode closer to have a look and was amazed by the green-blue water and the white glacier above. Soaking in the view of what he called Emerald Lake, Wilson later recalled, "As God is my judge, I never in all my explorations saw such a matchless scene."

The original Lake Louise village, a station along the CPR route, was opportunistically called Holt City after a CPR contractor, then Laggan after a village in Scotland. Then, in 1884, the area was renamed Lake Louise in honour of Queen Victoria's fourth daughter, Princess Louise Caroline Alberta, wife of Canada's fourth Governor General, the Duke of Argyll (Marquess of Lorne). Once again, the vision for Chalet (later

Castles, Crags, and Caves

Banff Springs Hotel, the "Castle in the Wilderness."
LIBRARY AND ARCHIVES CANADA PA-058051

Chateau) Lake Louise came from Van Horne, who wanted a "hotel for outdoor adventure and alpinists." And once again, it was made of wood. The simple one-storey log cabin, or "rustic chalet," included a central dining room, kitchen, office, and bar, plus two bedrooms, with large windows facing the lake. It too fell victim to flames in 1893 and was rebuilt in 1894. Yet another fire in 1925 destroyed all but one wing of the lodge. Again the hotel was rebuilt, but this time from more permanent material in a more impressive style. In its first year, the cabin registered a total of fifty guests, but by 1912 the expanded Chalet Lake Louise hosted fifty thousand overnight guests.

The Lake Louise Tramway was a hotel operation unique in Canada. The narrow-gauge branch line was built by the CPR to transport its summer guests up the steep grade from the Laggan railway station to and from the hotel. Prior to the tram being built, horse-drawn carriages took up to one and a half hours to climb the steepest part of the hill. Eventually, guest complaints about animal cruelty forced the CPR to shift to mechanical power. The 5.8-kilometre rail line followed a corkscrew route, crossing the Bow River immediately upon leaving the station, then looping back to cross Louise Creek and climb a steep 4 percent gradient to arrive at a turnaround loop at the hotel. The line was also used to move men and materials in during the winter months for construction work to expand the hotel. Truly, the incline at Big Hill that was tamed with Schwitzer's Spiral Tunnels had nothing on this mini-engineering creation. The original equipment, including two 8.5-metre open-bench passenger cars weighing 9.5 tonnes each, two freight cars for luggage, and gas engines for pulling the load, were delivered in 1912 and operated until service was discontinued in 1930. By that time, the Great Depression had reduced the number of guests, and better motor-vehicle access was available for those who did come.

* * *

The Columbia Icefield, the largest subpolar ice mass in North America, is constantly on the move, expanding, contracting, and shaping the local geography as it has done for millennia. The Icefields Parkway (a.k.a. Highway 93 North) parallels the Continental Divide, the backbone of North America that stretches 232 kilometres through Banff and Jasper National Parks. The Columbia Icefield was first reported by J. Norman Collie and Hermann Woolley following their ascent of Mount Athabasca in 1898. One of the largest accumulations of ice and snow south of the Arctic Circle, the icefield covers 215 square kilometres, reaching depths of up to 360 metres. Continuous snow accumulation feeds eight glaciers, including the Athabasca, Dome, and Stutfield, all visible from the Icefields Parkway.

The Columbia Icefield is considered a hydrological apex because its meltwater feeds streams and rivers flowing into the Arctic, Pacific, and Atlantic Oceans. The first trip along what is today the Icefields Parkway was made in 1904 through the high peaks northeast of Lake Louise by Jim Brewster, along the route aptly named the Wonder Trail. He later operated Great Glacier Trail horseback excursions for adventurers who explored the edges of the icefield near Castleguard Meadows, or were guided onto the glaciers on foot, with snowshoes, or on horses equipped with spiked horseshoes to better grip the ice. By 1981, safe and comfortable excursions on the Columbia Icefield at the Athabasca Glacier became available in the first snowcoach. Today, a fleet of massive Ice Explorer vehicles specially designed for glacial travel are operated by the company Brewster started.

But it was 1931 before construction of an auto route to the area was started. Crews worked from both the north and south to a meeting point near the Columbia Icefield. The initial gravel road penetrated old-growth forest dominated by Engelmann spruce more than four hundred years old, twenty metres high, and up to one metre in diameter. Given local climate conditions, these are surprising specimens, and stumps of trees cut to make bridge timbers are still visible.

The original parkway was built during the Great Depression as a work-relief project to create employment. Men earning twenty cents a day worked with hand tools and horses to build the route from Lake Louise to Jasper. The work was completed in 1939, and the first cars arrived in 1940. Today, modifications to the Mount Kitchener/ Sunwapta Canyon viewpoint on the Icefields Parkway include a 350-metre cliff-edge walkway and the Glacier Skywalk, a cantilevered, horseshoe-shaped glass-and-steel platform anchored in the mountainside. The Skywalk provides visitors with a soaring vista of the peaks, geology, biology, and changing ecosystems in the retreating glacial ablation zone. Built at a cost of $21 million, the project drew criticism from environmentalists for its possible negative effect on park wildlife and its commercial resolve to charge money for a view that had always been free. The engineering concept is similar to the Grand Canyon Skywalk, an aerial walkway located 1,219 metres above the Colorado River that was opened in 2007 by the Hualapai Tribe in Arizona.

The Grand Trunk Railway was another hotel builder. As a private company incorporated in 1852 to run trains between Montreal and Toronto, it was headquartered in England but received generous Canadian government subsidies. However, the railway became unprofitable because of competition from shipping and American railways. Against all reason, in 1914 it undertook, with its subsidiary, the Grand Trunk Pacific Railway Company, to build a 4,800-kilometre transcontinental link to Prince Rupert in northern British Columbia. The very expensive line was too far north of major population centres and had too little traffic to make it viable. But, imitating the CPR, the GTR built and operated a series of large hotels during the early twentieth century, including Jasper Park Lodge.

In 1813, a fur-trade outpost named Rocky Mountain House was established by the North West Company at a point between the Yellowhead and Athabasca Pass crossings of the Rocky Mountains. The post provided supplies and stabling for horses, and traded goods for meat and furs. In 1814, it was staffed with one interpreter, one horse keeper, two hunters, and two hired fur traders. In 1817, Jasper Hawes took command of the post, which became known as "Jasper's House" to distinguish it from Rocky Mountain House on the North Saskatchewan River. Within a few decades, the European demand for fur declined, and Jasper House was abandoned in 1884.

For the next twenty-three years, the area remained undeveloped, until the establishment in 1907 of Jasper Forest Park, later renamed Jasper National Park when it was granted national park status in 1930. Around that time, a group of surveyors from Grand Trunk Pacific Railway came upon the remnants of the original Jasper House and used the materials to build a raft. Then, in 1911, the Grand Trunk Pacific Railway arrived. A train station was built on the site of the old outpost and named for the company's first vice-president, Earl Hopkins Fitzhugh Jr. The Fitzhugh name did not stick, though, and reverted to Jasper within a few years.

To accommodate the railway crews, the GTPR built a series of ten large tents, with wooden floors and walls, along the shore of nearby Lac Beauvert. Tent City, as it became known, soon evolved into a luxury rest stop for tourists travelling on the Grand Trunk line. The large dining tent was converted into an evening recreation centre where guests who arrived by train played cards and chatted. In 1921, the site was further developed by Grand Trunk Pacific into Jasper Park Lodge. The resort comprised eight log cabins and was later expanded with additional guest bungalows and a main building proclaimed to be the largest single-storey log structure in the world. Like the CPR, the GTR promoted its resort in the Rockies as being in the "North American Alps." Here too, fire destroyed the main lodge, in 1952. It was rebuilt, and the original log cabins were replaced with cedar cabins. In 1923, the Grand Trunk Pacific Railway was absorbed into the Canadian National Railway. The lodge has lived on through different private owners as a successful resort, hosting thousands of visitors each year.

* * *

Another natural marvel of the Rocky Mountains is its abundance of hot springs. Some hot springs are located in resorts, some in picturesque national or provincial parks, and some in remote areas only accessible by hiking, paddling, or chartering a boat or float plane. The geological processes that raised the Rocky Mountains left deep faults in the rock. As snow high in the mountains melted, the water entered the rocks through these faults or fissures and ran deep inside the mountains, where it was heated by convective circulation at depths of several kilometres or more. Year after year, the process was repeated. After a long underground voyage, the water bubbled back to the surface, emerging much warmer than when it entered, to form hot springs in pools on the rock surface.

The first recorded reference to the Cave and Basin Hot Springs site near Banff was by James Hector of the Palliser Expedition in 1859. Later, in 1883, CPR employee William McCardell described the mist-filled cave in Banff's Sulphur Mountain to be "like some fantastic dream from a tale of the Arabian Nights." He, his brother, Thomas, and their companion, Frank McCabe, rolled a tree trunk through the cave's skylight entrance and climbed in to have a look. The next year they built a small shack nearby and prepared to cash in by opening the natural phenomenon to the public. But theirs was not the only claim, as the Macdonald government had also recognized the financial benefits of the Rockies tourist trade. A federal order-in-council in 1885 set aside twenty-six square kilometres as the Banff Hot Springs Reserve. The order stated that the springs would be forever "reserved from sale or settlement or squatting . . . " In 1886, a tunnel was bored into the Cave and Basin grotto to make access easier for visitors. The government held an inquiry into compensation for the various claimants, and McCardell and McCabe received $675. From their curative powers to their development as a naturally heated swimming pool to their designation as a national historic site in 1981, the Cave and Basin Hot Springs were Mother Nature's engineering marvel in the mountains.

In 1890, the first private ownership of Radium Hot Springs, in the east Kootenays, was registered to Roland Stuart for the sum of $160. By 1923, the new Banff–Windermere Highway was complete, and, once again, ownership of the springs was transferred into the hands of government and the first pool opened to the public. Hot springs continued to be developed in the high peaks at sites such as Ainsworth, Canyon, Halcyon, Halfway River, Nakusp, and Whiteswan.

Most of the precipitation falling on the slopes of Sulphur

Mountain in Banff National Park flows into the Bow River, but some seeps through cracks in the rock to a depth of three kilometres below the surface. As it descends, the water is warmed to the boiling point by heat from the earth's molten core and rises back up under pressure. How hot it gets depends on the rate at which it rises and the amount of surrounding cooler groundwater. The waters are warm at Cave and Basin, but hot at the Upper Hot Springs, the highest thermal springs in Canada at 1,684 metres. When water is heated, it acts to dissolve minerals from the surrounding rock. Pyrite and gypsum are two common sulphur-bearing minerals found in Banff's Sulphur Mountain hot springs. The rotten-egg odour (hydrogen sulphide) is produced when sulphate-reducing bacteria break down these dissolved minerals in the water before it surfaces. Phew!

Epilogue

ENGINEERING IN THE MOUNTAINS WAS a double-edged sword. Workers decimated whole forests to cut rights-of-way and harvest timber for trestles, ties, and poles. They excavated huge swaths of land, bored tunnels through mountains, blasted ledges into cliff faces, and redirected waterways. The deforestation caused erosion and altered water tables and catchment basins. Faced with impossible deadlines, engineers took shortcuts that resulted in death and injury to workers and, in the long run, led to higher costs and even greater delays. Routes chosen on the basis of expediency resulted in expensive repairs to locomotives, purchases of extra rolling stock, and a continual need to replace track washed away by floods or torn up by rock slides and avalanches.

Epilogue

On the positive side, more people could see more of their own country in less time and in greater comfort than ever before. Commercial development along transportation routes brought new opportunities and a higher standard of living to people in previously isolated regions. The variety and complexity of Rocky Mountain engineering initiatives provided thousands of high-paying jobs for labourers and skilled tradespeople. Manufactured goods could be brought in for a growing consumer class, while raw materials could be moved to national and international markets. And the high-peaks recreational experience was still there for all to enjoy.

* * *

The environment continues to exert an equivalent pushback on people. The summits have not been subdued. Nature is not fragile. Through threatening terrain, extreme weather conditions, and fluctuating wet and arid climate zones, the timeless forces of nature continually challenge human intervention. To accomplish their objectives, the builders of rail and road, trestle and tunnel had to adapt to the environment at the same time as they sought to manipulate it. They connected with the wonders and power of nature at a visceral level, and the outcome was a draw.

And the struggle continues. In 1886, while digging a well to get water for steam locomotives, CPR crews discovered natural gas at Alderson, Alberta, which was subsequently used to heat and power their station. Today, instead of rail and road, energy pipelines transport oil and natural gas from source to processing to distribution. Mountain pipelines are the engineering challenge of the twenty-first century. These winding networks of pipes cross the landscape both above and below ground, linking many areas of the country. Public opinion on pipelines is both loud and strongly divided. Many people see them as necessary to the maintenance of our modern societies; others view them as a blight with the power to do irreversible harm to the environment.

In Canada's new energy economy, the rush is on to forge pipeline corridors through the Rocky Mountains, as this is seen as the most efficient way of getting Alberta oil to port. Unlike the transportation routes of the past, these projects must undergo close public scrutiny before they can begin. Some current projects under consideration include Enbridge's Northern Gateway Project, a 1,177-kilometre-long twinned pipeline that would carry molasses-like diluted bitumen from Bruderheim, northeast of Edmonton, Alberta, to the Pacific Ocean at Kitimat, BC. Another is the proposed expansion of Kinder Morgan's Trans Mountain Pipeline that runs from Edmonton to the company's marine terminal in Burnaby, BC. The project proposes to twin the existing pipeline, which has been operating since 1953. A third major project is TransCanada Corporation's proposed 1,897-kilometre Keystone XL Pipeline. This advanced pipeline would carry up to one million barrels of crude oil a day

Epilogue

from Hardisty, Alberta, to Steele City, Nebraska, where it would connect with existing pipeline systems to reach refineries on the American Gulf Coast. Some have argued that Canada should be refining its own oil for its own use, but that is another story for another time and place.

Opposition to all of these projects is focused on the environmental impacts of pipeline construction and the risks pipelines pose to land, air, water, and wildlife. The economic forces that drive transportation development are as powerful as they ever were, but, unlike the railway and highway builders of the past, the engineers of today must confront a chorus of well-organized dissenting voices. The challenge of the future is for new engineering marvels that can bridge the distances between industrial development and environmental concerns.

Chronology

1807 Hudson's Bay Company explorer David Thompson surveys Howse Pass in present-day Banff National Park.

1813 The North West Company establishes "Jasper's House" fur-trading post in the Rocky Mountains.

1837 The American inventor Samuel Morse invents a system of code for transmitting messages across telegraph lines.

1852 The Grand Trunk Railway, headquartered in England, is incorporated to run train services between Montreal and Toronto.

1857 The Palliser Expedition begins a three-year survey of the North-Western Territory from Lake Superior to the Pacific Coast on behalf of the British government.

1858 The Cariboo gold rush begins in the colony of British Columbia.

1858 Sandford Fleming, a surveyor with the Grand Trunk Railway, reaches Yellowhead Pass in the Rocky Mountains and envisions a coast-to-coast national railway.

1859 The first parties of Overlanders, agricultural settlers from eastern Canada, leave Fort Garry (Winnipeg), headed for the goldfields of British Columbia.

1865 Walter Moberly, a road engineer with the Colony of British Columbia, discovers Eagle Pass in the Monashee Mountains.

1871 British Columbia becomes the sixth province to enter into Confederation with the Dominion of Canada, joining Ontario, Quebec, Nova Scotia, New Brunswick, and Manitoba.

Chronology

1872 The Canadian Pacific Survey is established under the leadership of Sandford Fleming to chart a course for a new national railway.

1877 Tribes of the Blackfoot Confederacy in Alberta sign Treaty 7 with Canada, establishing reserves for people of the Siksika (Blackfoot), Kainai (Blood), Piikani (Peigan), Tsuu T'ina (Sarcee), and Nakoda (Stoney) nations.

1879 Dutch-American engineer Andrew Onderdonk begins construction of the western section of the trans-Canada railway from Port Moody to Revelstoke, BC. The construction will take six years and pass through some of the country's most rugged and formidable terrain.

1881 The Canadian Pacific Railway (CPR) is incorporated and receives funding and land grants from the Canadian government to complete the trans-Canada railway.

1882 American engineer A.B. Rogers discovers Rogers Pass, the final link though the Selkirk Mountains that will join the eastern and western sections of the CPR.

1883 The rotary snowplow is manufactured by Canadian Orange Jull. The plow's huge steel blades attach to the front of the engine to scoop snow from the tracks.

1884 The CPR completes the Kicking Horse Pass section of the railroad from Lake Louise, Alberta, to Field, BC, including the infamous "Big Hill."

1885 Donald Smith (Lord Strathcona) drives the "last spike" in a ceremony marking the completion of Canada's transcontinental railway.

1885–86 The Canadian government establishes Banff, Glacier, and Yoho National Parks.

1886 The first passenger train from Montreal arrives in Port Moody, BC. The line is extended shortly thereafter to Gastown (Vancouver).

1888 Banff Springs Hotel is opened in the Rocky Mountains.

1897 The CPR constructs the Crowsnest Pass rail line to serve BC's farming and mining communities and protect the border from US railroad incursions.

1909 The Spiral Tunnels are built in Kicking Horse Pass, halving the grade of the dangerous "Big Hill."

1910 The CPR begins construction of the Kettle Valley Railway in southeastern British Columbia.

1914 The CPR begins construction of the Connaught Tunnel in Rogers Pass.

1921 Grand Trunk Pacific Railway opens Jasper Park Lodge.

1923 The Grand Trunk Pacific Railway is merged into the Canadian National Railway.

1924 The CPR builds the Big Eddy railway bridge over the Columbia River.

1939 The Icefields Parkway is completed between Jasper and Lake Louise.

1949 The federal Trans-Canada Highway Act mandates the construction of a national roadway.

1962 The Trans-Canada Highway is officially opened by Prime Minister John Diefenbaker.

1964 Canada and the US sign the Columbia River Treaty, opening the way to construction of the Keenleyside, Mica, and Revelstoke hydroelectric dams near Revelstoke, BC.

1984 The Mount Macdonald and Shaughnessy Tunnels are built to widen the route and increase the safety of road and rail travel through Rogers Pass.

Further Reading

Barter, James. *A Worker on the Transcontinental Railroad*. Cleveland, OH: Thomson Gale/Lucent Books, 2003.

Berton, Pierre. *The Last Spike: The Great Railway, 1881-1885*. Toronto, ON: McClelland and Stewart Limited, 1971.

Blaise, Clark. *Time Lord: Sandford Fleming and the Creation of Standard Time*. Toronto, ON: Vintage Canada, 2001.

Francis, Daniel. *Canadian Dreams: Myth, Memory and Canadian History*. Vancouver, BC: Arsenal Pulp Press, 1997.

Glazebrook, George Parkin de Twenebroker. *A History of Transportation in Canada*, Volumes I and II. Toronto, ON: McClelland and Stewart Limited, 1964.

Lavallee, Omer. *Van Horne's Road: The Building of the Canadian Pacific Railway*. Montreal, QC: Fifth House Publishers, 1974.

McDonald, Donna. *Lord Strathcona: A Biography of Donald Alexander Smith*. Toronto, ON: Dundurn Press, 1996.

Mitchell, David J. *All Aboard! The Canadian Rockies by Train*. Vancouver, BC: Douglas & McIntyre, 1995.

Pole, Graeme. *The Canadian Rockies: A History in Photographs*. Canmore, AB: Altitude Publishing, 1991.

Pratt, E.J. *Towards the Last Spike*. Toronto, ON: Macmillan, 1952.

Index

(Page numbers in italics refer to maps and photos.)

Index

Glacier Skywalk, 126
gold, 18, 44; gold rush, 13, 19; goldfields, 15, 17, 44, 45, 136
Gold Range, 93, 108
Golden, BC, 6, 27, 97, 109, 115, 116
Grand Trunk Railway Company (GTR), 21, 121, 127, 128, 136
Grand Trunk Pacific Railway, 39, 127, 128, 129, 138
Great Divide, 46, 73. See Continental Divide
grubbing, 10
HBC. See Hudson's Bay Company
Hector, BC, 75, 76
Hector, James, 41-43, 54, 129
Hell's Gate, 31, 32
Highway 3, 57, 65
Hope, BC, 6, 58, 59, 63, 65
hot springs, 129, 131. See Banff Hot Springs, Cave and Basin Hot Springs, Radium Hot Springs
Howe truss, 88-89
Howse Pass, 6, 46, 47, 136
Hudson's Bay Company (HBC), 13, 14, 19, 49, 47, 136
Icefields Parkway, 125-26, 138
Illecillewaet Glacier, 82
Illecillewaet River, 46, 93, 99
Illecillewaet Valley, 48, 49, 53, 68, 93
Jasper, AB, 6, 126,
Jasper National Park, 125, 128
Jasper Park Lodge, 120, 127, 138
Jasper's House, AB, 127, 128, 136
Kamloops, BC, 6, 28, 29
Kettle Valley Railway (KVR), 57-66, 61, 138
Kicking Horse Pass, 6, 41, 48, 51, 52, 53, 56, 70, 73, 74, 76, 80, 81, 86, 93, 116, 137, 138
Kicking Horse River, 42, 80, 116
Kootenay Lake, 112
Kootenay Landing, BC, 56
Kootenay National Park, 42, 85
Kootenay Pass, 41
Ktunaxa (Kootenay) First Nation, 47
Lachance, Billy, 100
Laggan, AB, 122, 124
Lake Louise, AB, 6, 73, 75, 77, 83, 84, 122, 125, 126, 137, 138. See Chateau Lake Louise
Lake Louise Tramway, 124
Lake Superior, 22, 25, 41, 107, 108, 136

Last Spike, the, 110, 111, 112, 137
Lethbridge, AB, 6, 56
Lethbridge Viaduct, 80
locomotive, 24, 33, 57, 64, 69, 75, 76, 77, 78, 85, 86, 89, 90, 100, 103, 132, 133
Lytton, BC, 32, 33, 35
Macdonald, John A., 21, 22, 28, 39, 107, 112, 130
Macdonald Tunnel, 70, 71, 72, 73, 138
Macoun, John, 48
Mallandaine, Edward, 110, 111, 112
McCulloch, Andrew, 59, 60, 62, 66
Metis, 107
Mica, BC, 96
Mica Dam, 96, 97, 115, 138
Mile One, 118
Mile 0, 118
Moberly, Walter, 46, 47, 48, 49, 53, 108, 136
Monashee Mountains, 6, 38, 46, 58, 91, 93, 108, 136
Mount Athabasca, 125
Mount Columbia, 38
Mount Deville, 50
Mount Hector, 43
Mount Lefroy, 84, 85
Mount Kitchener, 126
Mount Macdonald, 68, 70, 104, 115, 117; Tunnel, 70, 72, 73
Mount Ogden, 79, 80
Mount Robson, 38
Mount Rundle, 53
Mount Shaughnessy, 70; Tunnel, 72, 73
Mount Stephen, 74, 76, 79, 82; Tunnel, 74
Mount Tupper, 117
Mount Victoria, 85
Mountain Creek Bridge, 89, 90, 91
Myra Canyon, 60, 62, 65, 66
navvy, 27, 111; Navvy Peak (Table Mountain), 27
Nine Mile Canyon, 94
North American Cordillera. See Cordillera, North American
North Bend. See Boston Bar
North West Company, 40, 47, 127, 136
North West Mounted Police, 107
Northwest Rebellion, 107
North-West Territory, 19, 49, 136
Onderdonk, Andrew, 26-37, 52, 54, 91, 109, 137
Okanagan, 59; Falls, 65; Highlands, 58; Valley, 58, 59, 60

Ottertail Station, 74
Overlanders, the, 44–45, 136
Palliser, John, 40, 41, 44, *54*
Palliser Expedition, the, 39, 40–41, 129, 136
pipelines, 134–35
Port Mann Bridge, 95
Port Moody, BC, 23, 26, 29, 35, 111, 112, 113, 137
Purcell Mountains, *6*, 38
Quesnel, BC, 14, 45
Radium Hot Springs, 42, 130
Revelstoke, BC, 26, 33, 35, 56, 93, 95, 97, 100,
    101, 109, 115, 116, 137
Revelstoke Dam, 96, 97, 138
Riel, Louis, 107, 108
Robson, John, 18
Rocky Mountains, *6*, 20, 25, 26, 38, 39, 50, 67,
    73, 87, 91, 120, 121, 127, 129, 133, 134, 136,
    138
Rocky Mountain House, AB, 127
Rocky Mountain passes, *6*, 41
Rocky Mountaineer, 86
Rogers, Albert Bowman, 51–53, *54*, 55, 111, 137
Rogers Pass, *6*, 46, 56, 68, 70, 72, 73, 82, 83, 88,
    90, 91, 92, 97, 99, 101, 104, 115, 116, 118, 119,
    137, 138
Ross, Alexander J., 111
Ross, James, 90, 91, 92, 93
snowplow, 99; rotary, 103, 104, 137; wedge
    (wing), 103
Rupert's Land, 19, 40, 42
San Francisco, CA, 14, 17, 18, 26, 27
Savona's Ferry (Savona), BC, 33, 35
Schneider, Charles Conrad, 33
Schwitzer, Edward, 79, 80; Schwitzer Solution,
    81, 83, 85, 124
scrambling, 27
Selkirk Mountains, *6*, 33, 38, 46, 49, 51, 52, 53,
    67, 68, 69, 70, 85, 87, 91, 92, 99, 137
Shaughnessy, Thomas, 59. *See* Mount
    Shaughnessy

Shuswap, 44, 82; Lake, 35
Smith, Alexander, 111
Smith, Donald A., 22, 55, *110*, 116, 117, 137
Smith, Marcus, 47–51
snowshed, 59, 68, 73, 97, 99, 101, 102, 104, 115
spikers, 11, 111
Spiral Tunnels, 78, 79–82, 85–86, 124, 138
Stephen, George, 22
Stoney Creek, 89, 90, 91; Bridge, 73, 88, 90, 91
Sulphur Mountain, 129, 131
Surprise Creek, 88, 89, 90
surveyors, 10, 37, 39–40, 47, 52, 128
telegraph, 10, 18, 35, 105, 106, 112, 136
Thompson, David, 47, 136
Thompson River, 13, 15, 16, 36, 45, 58
Trans-Canada Highway, 33, 70, 73, 78, 79, 86,
    94, 95, 97, 114, 116, 117, 118, 119
trestle, 10, 29, 60, 61, 62, 87, 90, 101, 102, 121,
    132
Tunnel Mountain, 53
Van Horne, William Cornelius, 23, 24, 36, 52,
    53, *54*, 55, 75, 83, 92, 107, *110*, 111, 112, 121,
    123
Vancouver, BC, 47, 95, 96, 100, 101, 111, 113, 137
Vermilion Pass, 41, 42, 52
VIA Rail, 86
Victoria, BC, 14, 17, 18, 19, 111, 118
Victoria, Queen, 21, 122
wagon road, *16*, 18. *See* Cariboo Wagon Road
Wapta Lake, 43, 74
Whyte, Frederick M., 76
Whyte notation, 76
Wilson, Tom, 122
Yale, BC, *6*, 14, 15, 18, 29, 35, 95
Yellowhead Pass, *6*, 22, 39, 44, 47, 48, 52, 57,
    127, 136
Yoho National Park, 50, 78, 82, 83, 86, 137

About the Author

L.D. Cross is the author of numerous business and lifestyle articles that have appeared in Canadian and US publications. She has written many books in the Amazing Stories series dealing with unique aspects of Canadian history, including *Ottawa Titans: Fortune and Fame in the Early Days of Canada's Capital*; *Spies in Our Midst: The Incredible Story of Igor Gouzenko, Cold War Spy*; *Quest for the Northwest Passage: Exploring the Elusive Route through Canada's Arctic Waters*; *Treasure under the Tundra: Canada's Arctic Diamonds*; *Code Name Habbakuk: A Secret Ship Made of Ice*; and *Flying on Instinct: Canada's Bush Pilot Pioneers*. She is co-author with physician Marilyn Daryawish of *Marriage is a Business* and *Inside Outside: In Conversation with a Doctor and a Clothing Designer*.

L.D.'s creative non-fiction has been recognized by the International Association of Business Communicators' EXCEL Awards for feature and editorial writing and the National Mature Media Awards for her articles about seniors. In 2011, her book *The Underground Railroad: The Long Journey to Freedom in Canada* received the Ontario Historical Society Huguenot Award honouring "the best book in Ontario published in the past three years which has brought public awareness to the principles of freedom of consciousness and freedom of thought."

More Amazing Stories by L.D. Cross

Flying on Instinct
Canada's Bush Pilot Pioneers

L.D. Cross

print ISBN 978-1-927051-84-9
ebook ISBN 978-1-927051-85-6

Incredible stories of the brave and enterprising bush pilots who opened Canada's northern frontier.

Code Name Habbakuk
A Secret Ship Made of Ice

print ISBN 978-1-927051-47-4
ebook ISBN 978-1-927051-48-1

In the darkest hours of the Second World War, British and Canadian inventors team up to develop an immense and invincible new weapon for defending Allied ships from attack.

Visit heritagehouse.ca to see the entire list of books in this series.